Jean Chapman

DERBYSHIRE
WITHIN LIVING MEMORY

—•—

DERBYSHIRE

WITHIN LIVING MEMORY

Compiled by the Derbyshire Federation
of Women's Institutes from contributions sent by
Institutes in the County

Published jointly by
Countryside Books, Newbury
and the DFWI, Derby

———•———

First published 1996
© Derbyshire Federation of Women's Institutes 1996

COUNTRYSIDE BOOKS
3 Catherine Road
Newbury, Berkshire

ISBN 1 85306 399 1

The front cover, a charabanc outing c. 1930, and the back cover photograph were
both supplied by Mrs Shirley Aiton

Produced through MRM Associates Ltd., Reading
Printed by Woolnough Bookbinding Ltd, Irthlingborough

CONTENTS

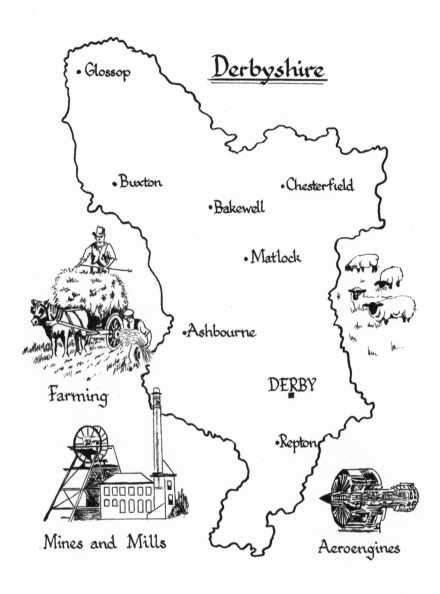

Derbyshire

Glossop

Buxton

Chesterfield

Bakewell

Matlock

Ashbourne

DERBY

Repton

Farming

Mines and Mills

Aeroengines

FOREWORD

We are delighted to share with you a picture of Derbyshire from the turn of the century to the 1970s through the memories of the people who lived there.

We often think that things were "better in the good old days", but I think you will agree with me when you read this book that times were often very hard except for the minority born into affluent circumstances. Derbyshire people saw enormous changes in their lives over the seven decades covered by this book. Industries such as coal mining declined and agricultural methods changed so much that far fewer people now work on the land. Improved transport facilities mean that many more tourists and holidaymakers visit the county.

We are very lucky to have this first hand record of people's lives as the 20th century draws to a close and I am sure many of you will treasure this book and pass it on to your children and grandchildren.

Patricia Rees
County Chairman

ACKNOWLEDGEMENTS

The Derbyshire Federation of Women's Institutes would like to thank the following members for their help: Anne Smith (Humbleton WI), the editor of the *County Link*, and her assistants; Winifred Astle (Sudbury WI) for the county map; Joan Ingram (Humbleton WI) for the delightful black and white drawings; Janet Joseph (Morley WI), our County Secretary, for typing the many longer entries; as well as all the WI members, relatives and friends for their interest and their memories. For reasons of space not every entry could be included, but without them all this book could not have been produced.

Shirley Aiton
Co-ordinator

TOWN & COUNTRY LIFE

MEMORIES OF
OLD DERBY

Memories of life in Derby between the wars, of the shops and the inns, the cattle market and the dairy.

◈ LIFE AT THE INN ◈

'I was born at the Robin Hood public house in Irongate, Derby in 1923. My father had recently left the army and he had to get good references to become a publican. I still have these, one from a clergyman, one from a lawyer and one from a well known Derby businessman.

My mother, one of ten children, had been brought up by her aunt, a childless lady. I believe it was quite customary in those days to "give" a child to a relative if you had a large family. Her aunt owned the Green Man public house in St Peter's Street, Derby and was a wealthy lady. I remember visiting her there as a small child with my brother. We would go upstairs and wait in the dressing room (one at the side of each bedroom) until we were summoned to the bedroom to see her. She was a very plain lady and very short and sharp to us, and we were always happy to leave, although we were always better off by half a crown, a great deal of money. Each Christmas she bought us an overcoat from "The Grand Clothing Hall" across the road in St Peter's Street. Her elegant clothes came from Kenneth Gregory in St James's Street and she was coiffed and manicured by James Swallow in the same street.

In 1924 my parents moved to the Rowditch Inn then on the absolute outskirts of Derby. I remember as a small girl drovers herding cattle down the main Uttoxeter Road to the Derby cattle market. They came from Mr Arthur Morley's farm in Mickleover. My father kept pigs at the back of the pub right until the 1939 war started and restrictions began. By this time the area was developing and Mickleover was a popular village, houses being bought by the "well off" business people wishing and being able to afford to move to this new suburb.

Next door to the Rowditch was a dairy kept by Mr and Mrs Stringer. Milk was delivered by horse and float by Mr Harry Radford and the only cleansing facilities were in a concrete outbuilding with a large tub. Water to clean the churns and bowls was heated in the kitchen. Milk and cream were sold from huge china bowls on the shop counter, and at weekends Mr Stringer made ice cream from the surplus cream. My brother and I still remember this ice cream and waiting in the yard on Saturday evenings for Mr Stringer to appear on the wall steps and give us any that was left. How disappointed we were if he did not appear for that meant it had all been sold.

Sometimes in the morning the local doctor's maid would cross the road to the dairy wearing black dress, white apron and cap and carrying a small silver jug. The jug would be weighed and then filled with threepennyworth of cream. Cakes were supplied to the dairy by Messrs Birds, in their very early days; they were often in the area and customers at the Rowditch. Mr Tom, Mr Reg and Mr Frank Bird were three lovely generous men liked by everyone and Mr Reg whom we knew best drove a large car, registration RC 33 – a tremendous status symbol in those days.

At eleven I won a scholarship to Parkfields Cedars secondary school and spent the rest of my school days there. My parents wanted the same education for both of us so my brother, although not quite the starting age, he was ten, was accepted at the opening of Bemrose School, across the road from our home. My mother served lunches at the Rowditch and quite a few of the masters came across for lunch. Bemrose School became used for Saturday sport and visiting teams came across to the Rowditch where they bathed and had tea. The bathing was done in the cellar kitchen; my grandmother came on Saturday mornings to light the coal fire under the copper in a brick building containing a cast iron boiler which heated the water to be used in tin baths and bowls. The confusion of steam, towels, water and raucous good humour I remember well! Tea was served upstairs in one of the public rooms and Grandma sorted the chaos left in the cellar kitchen.

Life continued at this pace until we left school and the Second

World War started to loom closer. I think the fact that the nation was at war came as a shock to the whole nation. We were supplied with gas masks and huge barrage balloons began to appear in the sky. Young men whom we had grown up with began to appear in army, navy and air force uniforms. As the war progressed we began to hear of casualties, lovely lads we had always known being lost on the ground, in the air and at sea. These things brought grief and sadness to everyone and people grew close to one another to bring comfort. Air raid sirens sounded as enemy aircraft approached, as although we were well inland, there was Rolls-Royce where warplanes were made, and the railway – a very large depot in those days.

As soon as my brother became 18 he joined the army. This worried my parents greatly and when my mother died very suddenly shortly afterwards we always felt that my brother leaving home at such an early age accelerated her death. My father and I continued to run the business, and as there were only two of us the extra bedrooms were allocated to army officers, and we did midday lunches for the staff of the Prudential insurance office, who had been bombed from their offices in Holborn, London and accommodated in a large local house. These jobs were interesting and we enjoyed them – we had an elderly helper who worked in the kitchen and in the bar. The kitchen was a cellar kitchen, the bar and eating rooms up a long flight of steps and the bedrooms up another flight from the public rooms. The officers had a sitting room on the same floor as the bedrooms, so it was long and tiring work.

In spite of all the sadness, grief and hardship which war inevitably brought, it was also a time of great camaraderie and support. The Home Guard patrolled the roads at night and always had a cheery chat and a joke for all they encountered. For a 18 year old girl, it was quite exciting – I met officers and servicemen and was invited to dances and functions, my father keeping an eagle eye on my activities.

There was great rejoicing when peace came, street parties and celebrations and the eventual safe return of my brother. Life slowly came back to normal until sadly my father died at the early age of 56 in 1950.'

▣ THE OLD COURT HOUSE ▣

'Very few people will remember the old court in the years up to the mid 1930s. The entrance was on the right-hand side of the main entrance to the Market Hall from the Market Place. The magistrates' clerk's office faced the Market Place and was next to the *Derbyshire Advertiser* office. The court was at the back and constituted a waiting room, court and magistrates' retiring room. It was then called "The Court of Summary Jurisdiction". The CID office was on the opposite side of the entrance to the Market Hall. It was very small. The Probation Service was in its infancy and the probation officers were called "Police Court Missionaries" at first. They had no office of their own but saw their clients in the actual court in the hour before court commenced.

I remember standing on a table in the office in August 1933 to see George V and Queen Mary passing through the Market Place on their way from Chatsworth to the Royal Agricultural Show which was held on the Municipal Ground, off Osmaston Park Road. At about that time Sir Oswald Mosley held a meeting in the Market Place and the large iron gates at the entrance to the Market Hall were locked with police on guard.

In the mid 1930s the new police buildings and court and magistrates clerk's office were built.'

▣ BROWSING ROUND THE SHOPS ▣

'I came to live in Derby when I married in 1952. My husband was away in the Navy so I used to often pass away the time by browsing around the shops.

I remember the devotion everyone had towards the Derby and District Co-op. My mother-in-law had me signed up before you could say "Jack Robinson"!

I used to shop at Sainsbury's in Cornmarket, with the black and white tiled floor and tiled walls. The manager wore a black waistcoat and a white apron. I seem to remember the apron being buttoned to the bottom button of his waistcoat.

I also recall the smells as I passed Hodgkinson's shop. You could buy everything under the sun there, and at Christmas it was full of all manner of delights. I remember shopping at Birds, which seems to have been in Derby since creation. When my family came to visit, a Birds pork pie was a must, and I still have to take one whenever I go and visit my brothers in other parts of the country.

I wonder how many people can remember the two large jars containing some unknown liquid, one bright yellow, the other blue. They were in the window of Cope and Taylor, apothecaries (1696). I was also mystified by the contents of the wooden drawers up the walls.

Do you recall little Janet who worked the lift at Barlow and Taylor's? It was a joy to be served by such well groomed and charming ladies.

Even on the coldest day the warmth came through from the stallholders at the Morledge Market, such a variety of stalls and their humour was amazing. I always associated Cockpit Hill with a shoe stall which sold pink fluffy slippers; another favourite place was the closed market, now so improved and still as busy. The old Fish Market amazed me, how did a town right in the centre of England, so far from the sea have beautiful fresh fish every day and such a variety?

I had my wedding reception at the Jacobean Cafe, I was so sad when it closed. I did at the time work for a short while at the Kardomah. Learning to make coffee was one of my duties and it had to be perfection.

We also made all those super meringues that were served in the cafe. They were cooked overnight, and it was the last thing we had to check before we left at night, were the ovens on at just the right temperature? A most important duty for me as the assistant manageress.

There are so many other shops I could mention such as Brindleys, Bracegirdles, Haslems and Clulows, not forgetting Bennetts. Thankfully all are still with us.'

'The Jacobean Cafe in the Wardwick opposite the library was a special place to meet for coffee, lunch or tea. They used white fluted china which I believe was made at Royal Crown Derby.

The Midland Drapery was another extensive store on the corner of St Peter's Street and East Street, a well known landmark and meeting place. On the front was a huge magnet

Shopping in Derby's East Street in 1948.

with the slogan: "To draw the people". The Midland Drapery was one of the places to go if you wanted your photo taken. They did Polyphotos – 48 pictures and all taken in slightly different poses. Some were dreadful but there was sometimes one which met with the family's approval.

Boots the Chemist was on the opposite corner. They had a library where you had the choice of A or B books. The payment allowed you to have a heart-shaped shield which was transferred from book to book.

The Picture House cinema at the bottom of Babington Lane was wonderful. Upstairs was a cafe and on Wednesday

Bottom Sadlergate, Derby, in 1948.

afternoons, when I went, you could order a tray of tea to be brought into the performance.'

'The Midland Drapery was a lovely shop to suit all pockets, but sadly it closed years ago, along with many others such as Barlow and Taylors and Thurman and Malins. Their Christmas Fairy Grotto incorporated a ride for the children and was super, with a present from Santa at the end. I remember, as a child, thinking we really did go on those trains and boats seeing the scenery going by, one year down in a submarine with fishes swimming alongside.

Another delight for children in pre-war years was to gaze in Ratcliffe Toys' window, situated at the Spot on the Osmaston Road. There was always a working train lay-out to watch with all the accessories.

The Derby Co-operative Society building skirted East Street, Exchange Street, Albert Street and Albion Street with many departments, with a cow on the roof of one of these buildings. They sold nearly everything, groceries, garden tools, fine china, shoes, ladies' clothing, and had a good cafe/restaurant and function room, with above the men's outfitters a bespoke tailoring on Albert Street. The system for payment in their shops, similar to many other big town shops, was for money to be put into metal containers and whisked away by vacuum power on an overhead track to a cashier point. One's change returned in the same manner.

Dividend payments were made to all shareholders on their spending, twice a year. At "divvy" times, there were very long queues up Albion Street to the Co-op office. You joined further queues once inside according to your share number. On submitting your share book you were given a voucher, then knowing how much in the pound the "divvy" was one could plan to spend this extra cash for Christmas presents or a summer holiday.'

▣ THE 1932 FLOODS ▣

'Markeaton Brook was culverted under The Strand and Victoria Street. It was not able to take the heavy rainfall and the culvert burst which led to flooding in Victoria Street and the Wardwick. Floodwater extended up St Peter's Street and towards the bottom of Babington Lane.

We parked our car at the top of Babington Lane and walked down passing the old Grand Theatre to see the floods. There used to be a plaque marking the height of the floodwater on the Whitehall Inn – owned by Pountain and Company, Wine and Spirit Merchants of the Market Place, Derby. There was a similar plaque on the walls of Strettons Brewery in the Wardwick. After the waters had subsided both the Midland Drapery and Thurman and Malins held bargain sales of flood damaged goods.'

SOME OTHER TOWNS
AND VILLAGES REMEMBERED

Thriving villages supporting all the trades and crafts we needed for everyday living, and a way of life hardly changed for generations – that was the world we grew up in. Here are a few memories of blacksmiths and lamplighters, chimney sweeps and bookies!

▣ REPTON IN 1910 ▣

'Repton in 1910 was very well served with shops. There were about 20 of them. At the square, selling haberdashery and a wide range of goods from bootlaces to cakes were Miss Pearson and Mrs Marshall, and in the High Street was Mrs Pentlow also selling haberdashery and gifts.

A Mr J. T. Taylor had two grocery stores and a bakery, one shop in the square, the other in the High Street in charge of a Mr Mee. At the rear was a large bakery where Mr Wimblett baked lovely cakes, buns and bread. Hot cross buns were baked early on Good Friday morning and were delivered to my home, Laurel Hill, by 6.30 am by Lionel Blunt. I was always given one in bed while it was still hot.

The larger of Taylor's shops was near the Pastures and at the front of the large window was a large coffee grinder so there was always a delicious aroma of coffee in the shop. The grinder is in a museum at York.

The forge in Main Street was a fascinating place where you could watch Mr Peach the blacksmith shoeing the horses and repairing or making many interesting items. The village school, dating from 1838, still exists. Next to it was the police station, with the lock-up and privy at the bottom of the garden. Next to that was the village hall, sadly since burned down. The hall was owned by Mr Arthur Turner and his two sisters. Mr Turner owned a talking parrot who used some very choice language when he was upset. Very enjoyable dances were held at the hall and the Metro Dance Band came from Burton to play. These dances started at 8 pm and finished at 2 am. The post office, kept by Mrs Pattinson, was also a grocery store, and at the side of the shop was the telephone exchange run by two of her family.

The Country Laundry is now demolished. It employed about 80 people, all from Repton and Willington. There were three horse-drawn drays and they made visits to all the surrounding villages and to Burton, Melbourne and Ashby. This could be very difficult in bad weather. It was a great thrill when my father allowed us to go to Melbourne on the dray. We took enough food for the day. It was against the law to travel on the dray, it was not for people. If we saw a policeman we had to hide between the hampers. Willow trees grew by the Old River Trent which ran near the laundry. The osiers were sold to a basket maker who lived in the square, he used to line up his finished baskets on the top of the wall. The wall remains, but no basket makers. We also had three garages, three butchers, two shoe repairers, a tailor's repair shop, a fish shop and a home-made cake shop.'

▣ THE SWEEP OF CRICH ▣

'My family went to live in Crich, near Matlock when I was six years old. This was in 1913, just three years after Florence Nightingale died. As a child I heard village people, who had known her, talk about her to my parents. When she was in residence at Lea Hurst, her family home in Holloway, she used to drive the three or four miles to Crich in her pony-drawn tub to visit a Crimean veteran and other sick people.

One of these was the village sweep, a tall thin, bent man, just a bag of bones, always dressed in sooty clothes. He was a good sweep, but he would come into the house, fasten his sooty bag round the fireplace, prepare the large sooty brush, then collapse in a heap on the hearth, moaning pitifully, until given a cup of tea, when he would suddenly revive and sweep the chimney expertly.

The villagers knew which day of the week Miss Nightingale

was likely to visit Crich, and the sweep listened for the sound of her pony's bell. When he heard it he rushed home, had a hurried wash and was in bed, groaning, by the time Miss Nightingale reached his cottage.

One day, so the story was told, he was a bit late hearing the bell. He dashed home, but had no time to wash, so when Miss Nightingale appeared, he was in bed, groaning, but with a sooty face.'

◈ SOME OLD DIALECT WORDS ◈

'We still use some of the old words so common in our youth. These were recorded at Old Glossop, taken down phonetically!

A ginnell was an alley; having a "gob like a beyler end" meant not being able to keep a secret; kecks were knickers; petty was the WC; razzart meant beyond repair; "sam owd" meant to take a firm grip on; "scutch up" was to clean up; slutch was mud and a "slutch pump" was a gully cleaner – or someone who drinks a lot of beer; "sod in trows" meant the grass growing in house gutters; swilker was to spill; and a tundish was a funnel.'

North Street, Cromford in about 1910.

▓ THE WRONG SIDE OF THE BRIDGE ▓

'There is a small stone bridge over the river Etherow. One side of the bridge is in the county of Cheshire. Cross over and you are in Derbyshire My father, a devoted Derbyshire man, used to tease me and say that I was born on "the wrong side of the bridge". However, all the lovely views from our cottage home were of the Derbyshire hills and so I grew to love them.

I only had to cross the bridge to be in Derbyshire fields. Many is the time we walked up Botany Fields and picked bluebells, buttercups, daisies and may-flowers (allowed in those days). Sometimes in autumn we went up Woodseats Lane and gathered a bucket (yes, a bucket) full of blackberries.

One of the highlights of our Derbyshire walks was to go through the fields to Gamesley. There we could watch the wonderful steam trains come chugging along on their way to Glossop and Hadfield.

Occasionally I walked all the way to Glossop town to meet up with two elderly aunts. These good ladies would have a real treat in store – a visit to a matinee at the old Glossop Empire cinema. There was, of course, no such thing as television, even a radio was rare, so a visit to the cinema was wonderful.

One of my happiest memories was sitting between these large ladies enjoying every moment of the early cartoons. All through the film my escorts took turns to enquire, "Mary, are you liking?" I always assured them that indeed I was!'

▓ MARKET DAY IN WIRKSWORTH ▓

'Market day in Wirksworth was a bustling time still in the early 1960s. Buses seemed to be everywhere and farmers came in from all the local villages. Public houses stayed open in the afternoon and the market stalls were full and always set out in the same way. Stallholders sold curtain material, clothes, fruit and vegetables, bedding and cooked meats. Howarths came from Belper and there was always a long queue at their stall.'

❖ THE GEORGE AND DRAGON AT WOODHEAD ❖

'This old inn, once a stopping place for the Red Rover stage-coach, was situated at Woodhead in Longdendale on the A628 Manchester to Sheffield road. As the village straddled the border between Cheshire and Derbyshire it was once a popular venue for illegal prize fighting – if the authorities of one county tried to stop the fight, the "sportsmen" simply crossed the border and continued in the next.

Directly facing the George and Dragon is the A6024 that climbs steeply over Holme Moss – a road noted for its perilous bends. The unique traffic sign at the junction – a skull and crossbones warning drivers of these bends – was painted by Eddie Bagshaw, for many years landlord of the inn. Originally from Eyam he had been a noted Derbyshire cricketer in his younger days. He was a great raconteur who would keep his customers entertained for hours with tales of Woodhead in the 1930s. There was the travelling fish and chip wagon for instance, that for want of inner tubes had its tyres stuffed with grass. And there was the "Professor" (one of the regular passing callers) who toured the fairs and shows of Derbyshire and south Yorkshire selling his patent pills for miners, guaranteed to remove the coal dust from their lungs. One evening when he'd had a drop or two more than usual he revealed his secret – the patent pills were made of boot polish, which had the miners who swallowed them spitting black for a week.

During the 1920s the George and Dragon became popular with Manchester University Mountaineering Club who nicknamed it the "Rope and Rubbers". It was here that the Mountain Rescue Association was formed. In 1928 the eminent brain surgeon Wilson Hey (a founder member of the MUMC) was climbing on nearby Laddow Rocks when a fellow climber, George Pryor, fell fracturing his skull and femur. He was carried on a makeshift stretcher down to the George and Dragon and thence by ambulance to hospital. Because of complications his injured leg had to be amputated. Convinced that the rough trip down from the crags had been a contributing factor, Wilson Hey put this point to his fellow climbers and so the famous rescue service came into being.'

⬚ Lighting up the Sky ⬚

'I was born at Little Hallam and recall Stanton ironworks at Hallam Fields literally lighting up the sky at night when the furnaces and cupolas were at full blast. While they were casting the pig iron, the smoke and flames would belch forth, while the river of red hot iron was poured in a steady stream down to the sand beds to make the blocks. No blackspot was found on rose trees in the district because of the sulphur in the air.'

⬚ The Bookies' Runner ⬚

'As a child in the 1930s, I remember seeing men on street corners wearing mufflers and cloth caps taking small paper packages from people passing by and putting them quickly into their pockets. Those packages were taken to a neighbour of mine, then the neighbour would ask us children to take a basket of them around to another neighbour in the next street. For this service we were paid one penny. This in the Thirties was a lot of money, especially for a child. I was a thrifty child and decided I would save my pennies. In those days we could get a form from the Post Office on which to stick twelve penny stamps and when it was full you could have two 6d saving stamps.

I told my mother nothing of my earnings until I had saved the shilling and then I proudly took home my savings book. My mother nearly had a fit. She explained to me what it was I had been carrying. I didn't know what a "bet" was but she told me it was against the law and that if I had been caught the policeman would have taken me away.

I then remembered that the lady I had worked for had been seen several times walking down the street with a policeman. Everyone in the district knew what she was up to, including the police. They used to take her in to be cautioned or fined from time to time. What they didn't know was that she used us children. That was stopped and I didn't add very much more to my savings. I hoped I had not been the one who had inadvertently shopped her, she was a lovely lady.'

❄ Snowy Days in 1947 ❄

'The big snow in 1947 for me by far surpasses any other memories of being snowed in. I was four years old and fortunately did not start school until after the Easter holidays. I lived with my parents at Atlow Mill Farm. The corn grinding mill had been driven by a big water wheel, so we were down in the valley with a steep farm track to ascend to get onto the road.

When the snow came the easterly wind blew the snow out of the fields, over the hedge, covering the track with about six feet of snow. Each day the cows had to be milked and the cattle fed. My father and Leslie our farm worker who lived in with us would go and dig away the snow from the farm track. I used to go with them sometimes using Mother's dustpan to dig with. They would dig all day until it was time to start the evening's milking and feeding. Each day we would get halfway up the track and in the night the east wind blew more snow back in, filling the track again by morning. This was no good as all our spare churns were being filled so my father made a wooden sledge for the big Shire horse to pull.

Because we couldn't get up the farm track Father asked Uncle Bill who lived at the next farm if we could take a piece of hedge out between our fields along the valley. Other farmers in Atlow did this and by working together were able to get to the main road at Bradley Corner – some two miles. By this time everything that would hold milk was full. The big tin bath, my baby bath, the big washday copper. Mother would have to make butter and cream cheese. I remember it hanging in a muslin bag from a hook in the kitchen. The whey dripped into a bowl underneath. Mother was proud of the fact that we didn't waste a drop. The milk went to Nestlé's dairy in Ashbourne but I don't know how we got the empty churns for we had no telephone to communicate.

It was five weeks before we managed to dig the farm track out and Father could get into Ashbourne in our Hillman Minx car with the aid of metal chains strapped to the wheels, for provisions. Snow was to fall again that night and we didn't get the car out again for another three weeks.'

'During the winter of 1947 the snow came at the end of January and stayed until the middle of March. Newton Lane at Bretby

Combs Road, near the Hanging Gate Inn at Cockyard, after the snows of 1947.

was filled to the top of the hedges with drifts and if we wanted to go to Newton Solney for our weekly game of badminton we walked in the moonlight over the top of them. My brothers dug out a road onto Knights Lane so that a tractor and trailer could take the churns of milk to meet the lorry taking them to the dairy and bring provisions in for the house.'

'On 14th February 1947 my uncle, who farmed 1,800 feet above sea level at Combs, discovered a number of sheep buried in a huge snowdrift and the only way he could reach them was via Long Hill. Two days before he had managed to get out of Combs with his tractor and open up a way for the delivery of 600 gallons of milk which had been held up on the farms. To rescue the sheep a party set off from Combs and arrived at Horwich End via Cockyard without much difficulty. They then proceeded up Long Hill where they found massive snowdrifts but their

Fordson Major tractor ploughed through.

Arriving at the nearest point to the sheep the three men and two dogs fought their way across the moor in an easterly gale and eventually reached the animals. For three hours they dug, and finally reached 19 sheep buried in a gulley and trapped. A few were in a state of collapse and had to be carried and the rest were driven to the waiting tractor and trailer. After a struggle they were safely loaded and the party arrived home eleven hours later. The sheep were coated in thick ice but after they had been put in the barn and fed, recovered. A day never forgotten.'

◙ LIFE IN THE DERWENT VALLEY BEFORE 1914 ◙

'My mother and father were in Derwent church at the "Watch Night" service in 1900 to ring in the new century. Both from old Derwent farming families, my father worked on his grand-father's farm and my mother was a pupil teacher at the village school.

Within the next few years life in the valley was to change dramatically; work began on the building of the Howden and Derwent dams, and a new "town" was built at Birchinlee some miles up the valley.

My father, the eldest of ten, left school at the age of 13. So many families in those days lost one or more children with consumption (TB) but all his family, save one who was killed in the Great War, lived well into their seventies.

The days were long and life hard on the hill farms. My father's chief responsibility was looking after the sheep and gathering them on the moors, although he had to take his turn at milking and looking after the other stock.

Butter was made from the cream and sold at market. Each farm kept several pigs which were slaughtered and salted down for the winter. Pig-killing day was followed by great activity in the kitchen; not a bit of the pig was wasted – brawn, offal, sausage, black pudding. What a feast! These would be shared with neighbours who would return the offerings when their pigs were killed.

Fairs were held at Hope (May 13th), Tideswell (June) and

Hathersage (October). My father walked sheep to Tideswell Fair some 15 miles away and then walked home at night. Hope Fair day was one of the highlights of the year and my father thought little of driving his sheep over in the morning, going home to milk, and returning to Hope for the evening's festivities.

My mother's family had, at the turn of the century, moved down the valley to a farm near the village. She became a pupil teacher at the village school at a princely salary of £7, rising to £9 and then £13 in the subsequent two years. She then moved on and had spells at Ashover and Grindleford schools before returning home to help her mother.

Her pride and joy was her Shetland pony and the governess cart in which she would take her mother out visiting or to Bamford station. The most usual form of transport at this time was the bicycle, although for group outings a wagonette would be hired. As a member of the ladies' cricket team Mother often travelled by wagonette and recalled how on arriving at a steep ascent the passengers had to get out and walk!

Light came from candles and oil lamps. Paraffin was brought from Bamford by a local trader. A tailor came from Bradford once or twice each year, and a local haberdasher from Bradwell visited every fortnight. Blankets would usually be ordered from the Yorkshire wool merchants who came each year to buy the annual "clip".

Clipping, or shearing, would take place in early June shortly after the sheep were washed in the river. Each farm would have a shearing day when 20 to 30 men would clip the sheep by hand. The farmer's wife would serve up two large meals – one at noon and the other at 6 pm. The shearers would return at night with their womenfolk and the local fiddler would play for dancing until the early hours.

Those days are now long gone and the farms have disappeared under the Derwent Valley reservoirs.'

◈ ALONG OLD ROAD, TINTWHISTLE 1910 ◈

'Tintwhistle fountain was at the bottom, given to the village when Edward VII was crowned. Further up was a butcher's shop belonging to Mr Jackson. From Lower Square there was a knocker-up – he would knock us up about 5.30 am to be at work in Hadfield by 6 am. At the bottom of Mount Pleasant was a wall with a very big stone on top called the Slurry Stone. This was where the stage-coaches stopped. Down Chapel Brow was a band room, and a hut opened by a man who sold clothes and bedding cheaply. He would buy things up from the pawn shop and sell them – shawls, clogs, button boots, blankets, quilts and children's clothes that had been made new for Whitsuntide and then pawned.

On Saturday night a greengrocer came from Ashton Moss, with rabbits. He sold five pounds of potatoes, carrots, onions and a rabbit for two shillings. He would skin the rabbit for you and buy the skin back for sixpence and we'd spend that on more vegetables.'

◈ BREADSALL AND THE BISHOP ◈

'Breadsall was a comparatively small village in 1935 with fewer houses than today. There were ten working farms mostly with

The King's Head Inn at Hilton – 'Good Stabling' was available earlier in the century.

dairy herds and arable land. There was very little traffic and the cows could be brought from the fields through the village at milking time. One farmer delivered milk straight from the churn and children loved going in the horse and trap round the village.

Our childhood was spent playing in the fields and woods around our homes. A great attraction was the blacksmith's forge. We loved to watch the blacksmith at work in a long leather apron shoeing the horses and one never forgets the smell of the red hot iron shoes when they made contact with the horse's hoof. The blacksmith was an important member of the community as horses were used on the farms and the Meynell Hunt used to meet regularly in the village.

Breadsall railway station was a lively place and was used for both passenger and freight services. There was very little road traffic and the children were able to have a skipping rope across the road, skipping and chanting "All in together girls, never mind the weather girls". Another popular game was "Jack of All Trades".

The Bishop of Derby had his residence in Breadsall and could be seen most days taking his constitutional with his wife. He would be wearing frock coat and gaiters very like a character in *Barchester Towers.'*

CHURCH AND CHAPEL

Sundays were special and marked a definite break in the working week for most families. Church and chapel were at the heart of village life, and the festivals high spots in the year. Most children attended Sunday school, and the annual treat was often the only outing they could look forward to.

◙ SUNDAY GENTRY ◙

'My father was a hawker at a time when hawkers were a lifeline, almost, to outlying districts. He had purchased a chestnut horse called "Jolly" from Hillsborough Barracks after the First World War. A beautiful horse who was a high stepper, beloved by the whole family and he was groomed to a satin coat.

Jolly might be reduced to the sale of pots, pans, brushes and dishcloths from Monday to Saturday, out in all weathers, visiting houses and farms along muddy tracks and badly made lanes, always quicker on the journey home to his loose box which was warm, dry and cosy in the adjacent field. But come Sunday, after church, Dad would don his three-cape driving coat, grey edged with burgundy braid, tall hat and a very impressive whip, and Jolly was resplendent in black patent harness, also edged with burgundy, and bright brasses. This regalia had been bid for and obtained complete with the matching trap from a sale at Mosborough Hall when a Mr Haddocks bought his first motor car. So moving along roads and lanes at a spanking pace with the family pet dalmations running between the wheels, the weekday workers became the Sunday Gentry, for no one could have been prouder than we were.'

◙ SUNDAYS WERE SPECIAL ◙

'In the 1940s and early 1950s when I was a girl, Sunday was a very sacred day. My father was the chapel Sunday school superintendent, so every Sunday morning off I went with him to Sunday school. On our way home we would call to see my grandmother who was usually just starting her lunch. Coming from Yorkshire she started her meal with Yorkshire pudding and gravy then had her "meat and two veg".

In the afternoon at 2.15 precisely, we set off again for Sunday school. If a local preacher came to take the service, then he would come home with us for tea – and we had to be on our best behaviour. I liked having a preacher for tea as we would have some nice cakes after our sandwiches and stewed fruit (damsons, plums or gooseberries) and custard. My father's brother had a farm where he kept a pig and managed to get fruit in the autumn to be bottled for winter. We also had hens at the bottom of the garden, so usually there were plenty of eggs, which in times of excess were put in a bucket of waterglass.

After tea, we all went back to chapel for the evening service. In summer we would have a walk before going home but in winter it was straight home down the dark lane and early to bed.

I was not allowed to knit, sew or listen to the radio on Sunday, something I did not like as I grew older and went to visit friends, whose parents were not quite so strict. In May it was the Sunday school Anniversary and I had a new dress for best ie Sundays and going anywhere very special. It was fun going to practice and calling at the chip shop for threepennyworth of chips in a paper and eating them on the way home. Again in the autumn when it was the Harvest Festival it was time for a new outfit. There were also plays to take part in at Christmas and Sunday school parties which were good fun.'

⬦ A TYPICAL VILLAGE PARSON ⬦

'Village life at Bretby in 1950 centred round the church and the parson of those days was a typical village parson – a bachelor, well educated and fond of his food and drink, jolly and well loved by both patrons and parishioners, and a familiar figure driving round in his two-seater Austin car complete with dicky seat. His care and concern for his flock, particularly in the immediate village area, was appreciated by all and he could be relied on to give support and comfort. He openly admitted that a day at the races was his great enjoyment. His premature death after over 30 years in the parish left a gap which has never been filled.'

⬦ THE HIGHLIGHT OF OUR LIVES ⬦

'My mother, though serious minded and business-like, had quite a sense of humour. An incident comes to mind when I was about nine years old. Every so often a talented trio came to entertain the Findern chapel congregation. A number of these stalwarts went round the circuit and it was our turn for such a visit. We all went along.

The male singer had a good voice and as the applause died down the master of ceremonies stepped forward to introduce a young woman. She was slight and held her small hands demurely in front of her. "She is now going to give you, in her own special way, a violent solo." The man emphasized the word "violent". I gaped at them, what was in store? I wondered how anyone so dainty could be violent. As she turned towards the piano I whispered to my mother, "Mum, what does he mean, a violent solo?" She shook her head, then the young woman came hurrying back carrying a violin. I exchanged a glance with Mother who was smiling broadly, shoulders shaking with suppressed laughter. It was a delightful rendering and needless to say not the least bit violent; however, poor Mother seemed to have a struggle to keep a straight face! We were so poor in those days we needed a sense of humour to survive.'

❖ WHITSUNTIDE ❖

'In Derby before the war Whitsuntide was quite a big occasion. It was a religious festival and on Whit Sunday it was customary to have new summer clothes to go to church in, although this was not always possible for everyone as money was short, due to unemployment.

On Whit Tuesday all the shops closed at dinner time. In various areas of Derby the Sunday schools met in groups in local parks for the Sunday school treat.

My memory is of Rose Hill Methodist church (now demolished) on Normanton Road. We were taken to Ambrose Street opposite the church where Offiler's Brewery stood. We were each given a coloured ribbon with the name of the church and date on it. The horses and drays would be lined up, all beautifully decorated with bunting; the horses even had coloured ear muffs. Barriers were fixed round the side of the drays and small seats put on for the young children. The drays belonged to George Eley, a coal merchant, who was a local preacher and a leading member of the church. The procession would form up, being led by the Boys' Brigade Band and the older children and teachers carrying the banners. The drays would follow. We would then proceed to Normanton Park joining up with other Sunday schools on the way. In all there would probably be eight or nine Sunday schools with around 2,000 children. A short service would then take place with representatives from the various denominations taking part.

After the service Rose Hill Sunday school would go down to the Memorial Ground on Littleover Lane. We were then served with sandwiches from the old-fashioned wicker clothes baskets, a cake and a cup of tea from urns – no squash or plastic cups in those days. Then we would play on the swings and have obstacle, egg and spoon and sack races.

It was a wonderful day; computers and expensive toys will never give modern children the magic we knew then in simple things.'

'Whit Monday was a very exciting day in the small village of Codnor Park. All Nonconformist chapels in the district had a society named the Band of Hope which advocated Teetotalism. It was on Whit Monday that all branches of the society, both young and old, converged on the Monument Grounds, so named from a stone tower, 70 feet high, erected in memory of William Jessop, founder of the Butterley Company.

The grounds were beautifully laid out with a lovely large Hall and a small sweet shop where we spent our pennies and halfpennies. Each Band of Hope would send either a dressed dray, drawn by horses, or a Maypole, to parade up the hill, preceded by several bands, to the ground. Some children had walked three to four miles from Ripley, Swanwick, Riddings and Selston.

My friend and I, from the age of six, and for several years, carried a large banner which read "I'll never marry a man who drinks" (let me say my husband is fond of a good cup of tea). Inside the grounds we joined in games and competitions and were treated to tea of sandwiches and slab cake.

To many of us Whit Monday holds many happy memories, and I for one, cannot ever remember a rainy day!'

◈ HARVEST FESTIVAL ◈

'I remember the excitement of helping to decorate the church at Longford for the Harvest Festival. On the Saturday morning I would get up early, find my bike and pedal there as fast as I could. The church would smell of chrysanthemums, a scent which still evokes the memory of Harvest Festival.

Most of the ladies of the village would be involved in decorating the church. We children were sent to fetch the water in big copper jugs from the pump in the stable yard. Longford church is right by the Hall and only reached by coming through the park which had Highland cattle in it. During my childhood the flowers were arranged in vases and jam jars with foliage like yew and ivy from the churchyard to disguise them.

If we weren't needed we explored the church, in the tower or behind the organ, places we weren't normally allowed to go. Or we played with the tassels of the Love Lies Bleeding that were part of the arrangement in the font. This was always done before we arrived, I think by the Head Gardener at Longford Hall. Then we might wonder how "Longford Harvest Festival 1958" got into the skin of the large marrow always put behind the first pew near the church door for everyone to see as they took their places. When I found out how it was done I was most disappointed, the magic had gone.

Towards the end of the morning we children would be asked to arrange the leftover fruit and vegetables wherever they could be used. We found places like the base of the pillars, in front of the choir stalls or behind the back pews. I have one memory of balancing piles of apples on the corners of the pillars above the congregation's heads and hoping through the service that the vibrations from the organ would dislodge the apples into some hat. Not quite what we should have been concentrating on at the Harvest Festival.'

◙ SUNDAY SCHOOL MEMORIES ◙
'Brookhill Methodist church in Stapleford played a very important part in my young life from the time I was taken, as a baby, by my big sister in 1929.

The Sunday school Anniversary was the first big event. The "sitting up" platform seemed to reach the ceiling. You started "sitting up" on the first row and as you got older, so you moved up a row. The choir and small orchestra were situated in front of the pulpit. Mother made my sister and I new dresses, usually shiny satin, with a sash tied into a large bow at the back, frills round the neck, hem and sleeves. Straw bonnets and white socks and shoes completed the ensemble.

For the treat, everyone walked a mile over the fields to Archers Farm. We had tea in the farmyard, followed by games in and around the barns, with the older children climbing the haystacks. We walked home tired but happy in the evening.'

'In 1924 when I started school at Staveley I was also enrolled at Sunday school. My friend Peg's great aunt was the superintendent, so we were very much drawn into all the activities of the chapel. Not only did we attend twice on Sundays, but we had to go to the Band of Hope on Wednesdays. Mother would not let me sign the pledge as she said I would only break it when I grew older. On Fridays the choir would give a concert at some other chapel. Usually on Saturday there would be a social evening at our own chapel.

Highlights of the year were the Anniversary and the Whit Monday treat. For the latter we were taken to a field nearby for games and sports. We were given a packet of sweets. At four o'clock we went back to the chapel and were given a free tea of potted meat sandwiches, brown bread, cake, jam tarts and cups of tea.'

▣ No More Frolics ▣

'About 70 years ago, my family were staunch members of the Primitive Methodist chapel in Alvaston. We children were expected to follow family tradition of morning Sunday school, afternoon ditto, and evening service.

My uncle Harry was Sunday school superintendent for many years. One morning the horrific announcement was made. In future, all children must go into the morning service after Sunday school. No more walks and frolics in the fields.

On the first Sunday, my cousin May, a well known tomboy (not Uncle Harry's daughter – he and Auntie Ruth had no children), suggested that we sit at the back of the chapel, run out after the benediction, and escape through the gates. Round the back of the chapel we ran as fast as little legs would carry us but alas, waiting for us was the angel of doom in the shape of my Uncle Harry, who had run round the other side. We were marched into chapel like a pair of juvenile delinquents, as we were in his opinion.

After that, it was *four* attendances every Sunday.'

GETTING ABOUT

From the early buses and cars to the well loved trams, from trolley buses to steam trains, life seemed more relaxed and even transport had a character all of its own.

❖ SHOTTLE EMMA ❖

'I know that Shottle Emma, as our local bus was irreverently called, was running in 1935, how long before that I'm not sure. Its journey started and ended in Strutt Street, Belper, and ran through Blackbrook, Shottlegate, Hazelwood and Farnah Green seven times daily. The timetable was unpredictable. It carried some of us to school in the mornings for a penny and was supposed to leave Strutt Street for the next journey at 10 am. There was nothing unusual in travellers putting their bags on a seat of the bus and going off to do more shopping and the bus wouldn't move until each person was settled in their seat.

The conductress would "deliver" newspapers by throwing them into the appropriate garden as they passed. One day I was travelling on the bus and when we got to the Triangle at Belper it stopped to allow people to alight and a man got on and asked the driver, "Is Lottie on t'bus?" Yes she was, and he went to the back and spoke to Lottie for several minutes. You had to laugh.

A notice in the bus said "This bus waits for the pictures" (that was the local cinema), usually at 9.15 pm. I believe Saturday nights were great fun for the young people. They'd go to the cinema and on the return journey would sit at the back of the bus and have a great time. All innocent fun.

When I got my first job at 14 my wage was 10s 6d a week. I'd hitherto paid a penny for the ride home but after a day or two the driver said, "You're at work now aren't you?" When I said yes he said, "In future the fare will be tuppence"! Happy days. The Trent Bus Company took over the route in about 1952.'

◙ THE PICTURE BUS ◙

'Mr Warrington of Ilam ran a bus on Saturday and one we called the Picture Bus. He would pack us in, the late ones often standing on the bus steps packed like sardines. He would shout down the bus: "Now you lads, get them wenches on your knees and make a bit more room!"'

◙ TRAMS AND TROLLEY BUSES ◙

'When I was living on Osmaston Road, I remember travelling to Derby on a tram. The trams ran on rails and were guided by a driver who stood at the front holding a big handle. The seats were of cane with patterns made by holes, and the passengers faced one another.

The trams were soon superseded by trolley buses. These ran on overhead cables, with a long pole from the bus to the cable. The poles had a habit of coming off, when the driver had to get a long stick and struggle to get the pole back on the wire, with much crackling and sparks from the electricity. The funniest thing I saw once was a driver who forgot he had changed routes, and went the wrong way at the Spot intersection. As the buses could neither reverse or turn, the passengers had to get off and he had to go on the complete round to get back to base!'

'On every 11 pm tram a letter box was chained to the stair rail, and the general public were able to stop the tram to post their letters.'

'It cost a penny on a Derby tramcar for me to go from the town to my old home. The wooden slatted seats never seemed hard.

Victoria Street, Derby in 1948 when trolley buses were a popular form of transport.

Their backs were pushed into the reverse position by the conductor before the jouney back. I remember the sound as he went down the length of the car – slam, slam, slam. At the top of the tram were seats in the bay at the front and rear over the driver's compartment, near the top of the stairs. We children always tried to reach these seats before anyone else got there.'

■ SWOPPING CARS ◈
'My uncle had a car, which he needed for visiting farmers for his

Off for the day by charabanc. The cover could be pulled over if it rained.

job. One day he came back in a different car. He had swopped with a total stranger on his journey after they had started a conversation and discovered they liked each other's make of car – they changed over there and then. There was no paperwork, no registration papers involved at all. My cousin and I were delighted as we could now travel in the dicky seat at the back, well wrapped up in our scarves and rugs.'

◙ RAILWAYS IN THE PEAK ◙

'The Midland Railway led to Buxton from Manchester, and then through the scenic area of the Peak, passing through Millers Dale, across the viaduct at Monsal Dale, to Longstone, Hassop, Bakewell towards Matlock. It was a very busy goods line as well as providing a fast passenger service pulled by steam engines such as the *Hawkins*, *Somaliland*, *Iron Duke* and later, with the *Palatine*, to Derby and on to St Pancras.

Special excursion trains took walkers to Bakewell, for walks arranged by the Ramblers Association, and to Bakewell Agricultural show in August. From Buxton station passengers were bused by North Western to Chatsworth, and the slow train stopped at Matlock Bath for Venetian Nights, in the autumn.

We used to catch the "slow" train to Derby from Bakewell station, buying a ticket at the ticket office before crossing the line by the little bridge. In winter there was a coal fire in the gas-lit waiting room, and in summer the flower beds outside were always well tended, as were all the station gardens along the route. There were always porters on the station and often railway workers travelling home on the train. The early steam engines pulled non-corridor carriages, and you had to put the window down before opening the door from the outside, to alight.

On the way to Rowsley station there was just a glimpse of Haddon Hall, before going through the 1,058 yard long tunnel (built so that the Duke of Rutland would not see the trains from the Hall). You could see rabbits in the fields, and bluebells in the spring.

Rowsley station had a very large goods yard with sidings, extending right to the A6. It was a busy place, and interesting to the railway enthusiasts. It housed the Express dairy, which always had steam rising from it. Local milk was sent all over the country by rail in large tankers after pasteurization and other treatment there.

The passenger stations at Rowsley and Hassop were both

rather opulent, as they were sometimes used by the Dukes of Devonshire and Rutland, and by the Royal Family, while visiting Chatsworth.

Alas, under the Beeching cuts this lovely railway was closed in March 1967, and the sidings at Rowsley before then, and of course the Express Dairy. Trains ran only from Matlock to Derby.

Thanks however to the enthusiasm and hard work of the "Peak Rail", a voluntary group formed in 1975, it is possible to travel by steam train to Darley Dale, and plans are going ahead to get to Rowsley and beyond – may they succeed.'

❋ MEMORIES OF MILLERS DALE ❋

'My memories of Millers Dale station are mainly of Platform 5, from which two coaches drawn by a push-pull engine carried children to school and adults to work in the spa town of Buxton. The train operated every 30 minutes at cost of sixpence. On this five and a half mile journey the train crossed the river Wye eleven times. On Thursday and Saturday stops were made at Blackwell Mill halt to enable housewives from the six cottages there to go to Buxton for their weekly shopping.

Millers Dale was so named because there were two corn mills beside the river Wye. It remained a remote spot until 1862 when the Midland line linking London, Derby and Manchester was laid. Forty years later, the volume of traffic necessitated an increase in the station area from two to four running lines and five platforms.

It was a busy junction for Buxton and a station for Tideswell. Business people, travelling by express train, reached Manchester in less than an hour; London was reached in three hours and ten minutes, and the trains were always on time!

The railway line created accessible transport, previously horse-drawn, for three local cotton mills, carried coal, the essential fuel, and limestone from the quarries, and provided transport for farmers. I well remember we had two cheese presses and a butter churn in the farm kitchen. When raw (unpasteurized) milk could be transported by train to Manchester Dairy Company, cheese and butter making ceased.

41

Motorised transport to the station greatly increased its activity, so much so that a permanent restaurant and a newsagent's stand flourished on the middle platforms.

The stationmaster wore two hats, those of stationmaster and postmaster. The post office, installed in the office, was sufficiently active to include the employment of two telegraph boys. Employment radiating from the station covered shunters, linesman, plate layers, signalman, ticket collectors and other station staff. Engine drivers were based in Buxton.

The only time the station ceased to function was during the 1947 snow when the line to the north was temporarily blocked. The first diesel engine, numbered 10,000, made its trial run from Derby to Manchester. Trainspotters from a wide area collected on the station to watch it pass through.

The Beeching cuts closed the station in 1969 and ended all the employment involved. How wonderful it would be to turn the clock back, and for half a crown return ticket, be transported by train on Saturday night to watch Alicia Markova and Anton Dolin performing at Manchester Palace Theatre.'

HOUSE & HOME

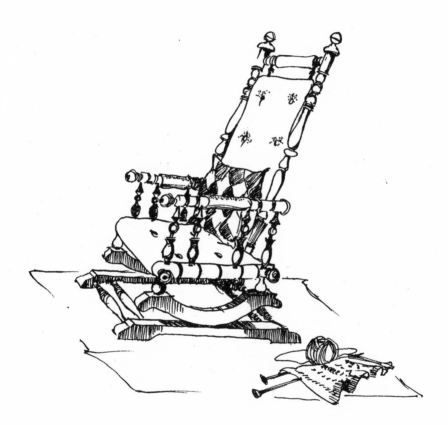

THE WAY WE LIVED THEN

Memories of farm cottages and little terraced houses in town, of the days before electricity and modern conveniences, of hard work and earth closets at the bottom of the yard – the way we live has changed so much.

▣ LIFE ON THE FARM ▣

'I was born at Kirk Ireton, number eight of eleven children, six boys and five girls, on a 21 acre farm belonging to the Blackwall Estate. My mother ran the farm and my father worked as a forester on the estate. I went to school, along with my brothers and sisters, at Hulland Ward, a two mile walk each way. On rainy days we would sometimes be allowed to dry our outer clothes near the coke-burning stove in the classroom, otherwise we sat and steamed. We took sandwiches for lunch, sometimes banana ones, which would be dark brown by the time they were eaten, and a flask of tea. Our father came home for lunch, but we children only had a "scratch" meal when we got home, and if it was a "proper" dinner, a large pudding would be served first to fill us up.

We slept four to a bed, two at the top, two at the bottom. Each bedroom had a candle and a potty. Teeth were cleaned with salt, which had been bought in blocks and then hacked into slices and crushed with a rolling pin.

The front parlour was used once a year, for the rest of the time we lived in the big kitchen. It had a range with an oven on one side and a hot water tank the other. My mother made bread, and it always tasted better when wood, rather than coal, was on the fire.

Most of our food was produced on the farm. There were eight cows, and surplus milk was taken by a neighbour to Shottle station and thence to Nestlés dairy. Our mother and father went by pony and trap to Derby once a week, and the horse would be

Going out for the day was by pony and trap until the first cars gave families new freedom.

tied up at the Central Stables, Cockpitt Lane (now a car park). They took eggs, potatoes and mushrooms to sell to friends, and what meat we ate was bought with the proceeds. My father bought hops, black treacle and sugar, and brewed beer at home. Each of us children would be taken to Derby once a year, usually for a birthday, and a special treat was to go to the teashop on the upper floor of the Market Hall and have a vanilla slice.

All the children were born at home, attended by a midwife. When I was old enough, I was "lent out" to act as nanny to various neighbours when they had a new baby. Two years after leaving school, I thought myself fortunate to be able to escape, and go into service at the Laurels, Ashbourne, the home of Mr and Mrs Atkins – he was manager of the Nestlé factory.'

❈ A MODERN HOUSE ❈

'I was born in 1919 after the end of the First World War. The world has changed since then. We had a "modern" house as it was known, outside toilet and no bathroom. Bath night was the tin bath in front of a big fire, with our clean clothes warming on the clothes maiden, and afterwards we had to empty the bath in the sink and dry it and hang it up in the cellar. This took place on a Friday night so as to be clean for the weekend and Sunday school – that was special.

Monday was washing day. We always had bubble and squeak and cold meat for dinner because Mum was busy keeping the set boiler going with coal, rubbing the clothes on a washboard, blueing the whites and starching the collars, and leaving Dad's overalls to the last – he was an engineer and started work at 7.45 am each day. The next job was scrubbing the floor and finally swilling the yard. This took most of the day.

Tuesday was ironing in the morning with two flat irons heated on the fire and a rubbing cloth to keep them clean. The afternoon was for shopping. Mum used to go to the butcher's first and pay for the week's meat and order some for the weekend. It was delivered on Friday by a boy on a bike, dressed in a long apron and wearing a hat. Next, to the Maypole grocer's for butter made into a pat with two wooden hands, and parcelled up and tied with string with a loop for your finger.

Wednesday was upstairs day – the beds were changed and everything polished. Rugs were brought down and batted with a bamboo plait and brushed, windows cleaned and the chamber pots disinfected with carbolic.

Thursday I loved. It was baking day. The smell of freshly baked bread, made into cottage loaves, lovely Dundee cake for Sunday, squashed fly cakes, parkin and sponge cakes fit for angels, apple pies and Bakewell tarts (not puddings in those days). Our garden was full of fruit bushes so we had blackcurrants, raspberries and rhubarb pies in season.

Friday the greengrocer came with his horse and cart. Bonny the horse knew Mum would have a carrot and a piece of sugar lump. He chewed away while Mum chose her vegetables for the weekend.

Saturday was market day. Dad went to football while Mum shopped. She bought some cream cheese wrapped in a piece of white linen cloth. It was delicious, we had it for tea. Then we sat around listening to the wireless – it was Dad's hobby, he was a wireless ham, making sets and winding coils. The neighbours came in to listen, then he made them a set. We had our own earphones – it was magic!'

▧ A MODEL FARM ▧

'Soon after marriage to a local farmer I moved into Home Farm, Bretby. Up to the 1920s the farm had belonged to the Chesterfield Estate and it had been a model dairy farm for Derbyshire, so the pride and joy of Home Farm was the marble dairy in the house to which Lady Chesterfield had walked every morning to drink her glass of fresh milk. Floor shelves and thrawls were of beautiful Italian marble but the meagre rations received by just two people in 1950 looked very lost in such surroundings. The Victorian fireplaces and big black kitchen range were quite awe inspiring and the arrival of the modern solid fuel cooker was greeted enthusiastically. The removal of the hooks in the kitchen ceiling marked the end of hams hanging to cure but the lead lined sink in an outhouse remained a permanent reminder of pig killing days. The game larder and back kitchens and the row of brass bells were also a reminder of the time of servants and hired hands.'

▧ A TERRACE IN DERBY ▧

'Most houses in Derby in the 1920s were terraced, with a black-leaded range. This had a centre deep fire excellent for toast, with an oven on one side and a boiler on the other. Most took about four gallons of water and had to be filled with a bucket and emptied with jug or ladling can. Odd ones had a tap, woe betide the person who took out the water and forgot to put it back. No electric blankets but an oven sheet or brick warmed in the oven and wrapped in a towel was very comforting. Most houses had gas but only in the two main downstairs rooms and the main bedroom. Other rooms used candles. Electricity came around 1928 (as I remember) but the wires were covered with a case over the wire and not with wires inserted inside the plaster.

47

Irongate, Derby in 1948.

Lavatories were commonly at the bottom of the garden with "nightmen" emptying the buckets on a set night each week. Toilet rolls were scarce or non existent. The commonly used paper was squares of newspaper or pages cut from magazines threaded on a piece of string. We had a water closet about 1929, still outdoors as there was no spare room to convert but it was attached to the house.

There were very few baths in the terraced houses at this time. In fact, only cold water. My grandmother's house, two doors away, still had the old pump although she had a cold tap. Baths as children were taken in front of the fire with my brother, youngest, being bathed first and me, the eldest, bathed last with just the addition of more water. Later each had a bath in the kitchen with water heated in the coal copper and warmth from the gas oven with the door open. Later still for one penny we could have a bath at Reginald Street baths with a measured amount of water, plus soap and towel. For threepence one could have a bath with taps and add more hot water as desired. The penny bath was quite adequate and warm enough.'

▣ TEA LEAVES ON THE MAT ▣

'Friday was cleaning day in the kitchen. The stove was blackleaded, then tea leaves were spread over the coconut matting to lay the dust. This was swept with a hard brush, on one's hands and knees, and when the dust had settled about an hour later the furniture could be dusted.'

▣ BEFORE ELECTRICITY ▣

'As we lived out in the country between Chapel-en-le-Frith and Dove Holes we did not have electricity until 1955. Prior to that the lighting was oil lamps which had a wick dangling into a container containing paraffin with a glass chimney, and generally stood in the centre of the table. We also had an Aladdin mantle-type paraffin lamp which gave a brighter light and threw out a lot of warmth. I saved up my pocket money to buy a Bialaddin lamp which had a handle on it so that it could be carried around and I could hang it in my bedroom.

Ironing was done with a flat iron heated on a good red fire and then a chrome shield was attached. Baking was done in a coal oven belonging to a modern "bungalow" range which also had a back boiler to heat the water. Breakfast was cooked on a small green paraffin stove which stood on the table. Washing was either done by hand, or using the copper boiler which had to have a coal fire lit underneath. The radio ran off an accumulator which we took to a garage to have recharged. There was no fridge only the cold pantry.'

'We had fires with side boilers and ovens efficiently heating the living space, the water, and constantly boiling kettles and cooking all the food for the family. Sometimes on a Saturday night the fire was made up and a piece of beef put in the oven in a dish with a lid, then the tenderest, most flavoursome meat was eaten with bread for breakfast on Sunday morning. All houses in Youlgreave in the 1920s and 1930s had paraffin lamps and candles bought from a hardware man who came around the village. My family had electricity very early on, very rare in the 1920s, due to my grandfather buying a dynamo powered by battery. He brought it home on a waggon and fixed it himself. An elderly gentleman in the village recalls that only his father was allowed to switch the light on when they first had electricity put in.'

❖ SCRUBBING THE FLAGS ❖

'My grandmother lived at Rogulum Cottage, Cromford in the 1920s. I remember the pantry floor with sandstone flags. She

Rogulum Cottage, Moorside, Cromford in the early years of the century.

50

kept them clean by scrubbing them then using a donkey stone on the edges to make them white. In the morning she wore a hessian apron and a long dark skirt, and in the afternoon she changed to a white starched apron.'

◈ THE COAL FIRE ◈

'As in the majority of homes, ours at Morley was heated by coal, and I suppose many people still cooked on coal ranges, though newer properties were cooking electric. We had fireplaces in both downstairs rooms and a small one in the main bedroom, but the fire was only lit in that if someone was ill in bed.

The coalman came fortnightly, usually with five bags, but some people could only afford a couple at a time. Coalmen always had black faces and hands, and left dirty fingerprints all over the doors and the cups from the tea which my mother always provided, and there were dusty footprints all down the path. When they'd gone, we always had to rush out and pick up the pieces of coal dropped in the road, before somebody else did. Those people with coal cellars often had their coal left on the pavement, for walkers to go round or trip over.

The chimney sweep was another dirty-faced visitor, several times a year, not at all like today's smart, clean vacuum sweep. The sweeping day was fraught, as there was always a lot of mess and it took most of the day to clean up afterwards. Everything was coated in a thick layer of soot, and it found its way into every nook and cranny. Chimney sweeps, like black cats, were supposed to bring luck to newly-weds!

As well as coal, the slack was made into briquettes to eke out the coal ration and all firewood was cut up very small to make it go further.

With everyone using coal, including many factories, there was a smoky atmosphere, increasing in foggy weather to "smog". It was in the days before the smoke abatement laws and everyone had bonfires too at the bottom of their gardens to burn their rubbish.

Our house was nearly always cold and draughty, unless we were sat directly in front of the fire. Making toast on the fire was

51

a good winter evening activity. Toast has never tasted so good from the grill or toaster. To go to bed, or to the bathroom, was like going to the Arctic. I couldn't have survived without a hot water bottle. Unfortunately, that usually lead to chilblains from which I regularly suffered every winter. Many houses were damp and a lot had cellars which became waterlogged in wet seasons. No wonder there were many chest problems.'

◙ ONE ROOM ◙

'When I was small money was tight. My father had just returned from the war and we had to live where we could.

We lived in a tenement house. Two familes lived upstairs, my family downstairs, and another family lived in rooms in the yard. My parents, my small brother and I had to share one bedroom, with one other room to live and cook in. There was no running water, we used a standpipe at the bottom of the yard and there was only one toilet for everyone to use. Yet despite this, there was a lot of community spirit around then, with everyone helping each other in times of need. I loved and still remember the happy times I had there as a child.'

◙ GETTING BY IN THE 1960s ◙

'For some months between 1963 and 1964 my husband, myself and our baby daughter lived with my father-in-law in a house which had been built in 1900. Very little had changed in all that time. It had been decorated in the 1920s when electric lights and a few sockets were put in. The lavatory did flush, but it was out in the yard.

The living room boasted an old range, but the water boiler leaked, and the oven did not work. The scullery contained a gas cooker made in 1900, which must have been a miracle of modern science when it was new, but it had seen an awful lot of wear and tear since then. When I lit the oven to try to cook a roast, the sides caught fire and flames and smoke gushed into the room. The fastest ring boiled a kettle in 20 minutes. It didn't have a grill. There was only one cold tap in the house, a high tap over a very low earthenware sink. I could boil water on the range but this was also slow. One day I drew the hood over the grate to try to make the sluggish fire burn more brightly, and set the chimney on fire. Fortunately the Fire Brigade were very good and did not leave *much* mess. I redecorated the living room, I could only afford lining paper and one coat of paint, but even that brightened it up!

The small engineering business which my father-in-law had inherited from *his* father had happily supported one man with modest tastes, up to 1963, but with our arrival resources had to be stretched to pay for the needs of four, plus a dog and a cat. Food and household necessities used to cost me about £3 10s per week, I believe the average at that time was nearly £7. I cooked all the cheapest meats in a pressure cooker, with lots of vegetables. This cooker, a wedding present, was my salvation, I could never have got the meals on time without it. One of the dishes everyone liked was a stew of ox hearts, another, fishcakes made of cod's heads. This was great to start with, as the heads were free, but when I wanted them regularly, the fishmonger started to charge! Heavy puddings and bread and marg filled the gaps.'

◙ THE EARTH CLOSET ◙

'Many houses in Willington had an earth closet in an outbuilding and the "muck cart" used to come round weekly at night. The man with the cart was called "Little Billy". If they missed any week Dad had to empty the loo in a pit in the garden. The polite name was "night sludge".'

'Our toilet at Ashopton was about 50 or more yards away from the house up some steps and along a path. If it was dark we had to take a candle in a lantern, if wet or cold sometimes wellies were worn. There was no toilet paper, but newspapers and copies of a magazine were in there, so we could have a read while sitting.'

'My grandmother lived in a large house in Chellaston, and outside there was a toilet with two holes in a wooden bench seat. My sister and I used to go together, she used the large hole and I used the small one. Granny would have a special roll of nursery rhyme toilet paper for us to use and we used to unroll it to see if there were any new rhymes.

As we walked home over the fields to Alvaston we would unfold our brown paper carrier bags with the string handles and collect dried cow pats to make manure for our home-grown vegetables.'

WATER AND WASHDAY

Water had to be fetched from wells or springs, and every drop was precious. Washday, always on Monday, used gallons of it and was a full day's work for an already hard working housewife. Baths, of course, were also weekly affairs and the whole family would often share the bathwater.

▣ WELLS AND SPRINGS ▣

'Many people at Youlgreave had no water in their homes and it was a common sight in the 1920s to see people drawing water from the taps near the wells, of which there were quite a few.'

'We lived in a cottage on the top of the hill on the Nightingale Estate in 1918. There was no water laid on. There was a spring about a third of a mile away and the children took turns to fetch the water. A ten gallon tank was used on a barrow as the journey was uphill to the cottage. There was a rope to pull at the front and someone pushed from behind. As you can imagine, there were many mishaps and plenty of spilt water. Our next door neighbour was more enterprising as he had a pony and cart and had tubs that he placed in the cart.'

▣ EVERY MONDAY ▣

'Washday in the 1920s was Monday. Every Monday and all day long. The huge copper in the kitchen was filled with some eight gallons of water, brought indoors in buckets from water butts in

PURE WOOL UNDERWEAR

Winter weight, made in England. Vests with long or short sleeves; ankle length Pants. Sizes 34 to 40 in.
SPECIAL PRICE
per Garment **6/11**

WINTER Dressing Gown

In plain Grey, Brown, Fawn, and Lovat, trimmed and corded in harmonising effects. All sizes up to 44 in. chest.
SPECIAL PRICE **35/-**

No easy care fabrics in the 1920s to help make washday easier.

the farm yard. In a hot summer this water had to be collected from troughs at a spring some distance away and transported in old milk churns on the farm cart. Soap would be shredded into the water and some soap powder – I seem to recall Rinso – was added and also a little soda.

Sticks and paper were laid beneath the boiler. These were then lit with red hot coals brought from the Yorkshire range in the living room. Eventually the water boiled and in went the washing. This had been previously washed in a dolly tub – quite a large galvanised tub with ridged sides. A dolly peg and a posser was used to agitate the clothes to clean them. I recall my mother always turned the dolly peg 50 times back and forth. Thinking about this, it was certainly one way of working off bad feelings.

The dolly tub had its constant companion – a mangle through which the clothes would go many times. There was a large galvanised bath filled with clean water to rinse the clothes and another small one with "dolly blue" water to make the whites appear whiter. Also a bowl of starch was made up for collars, tablecloths and pillowcases. After each process the clothes were mangled. Lastly they were placed on a line in the farm yard to dry in the air until one day a cow attacked the washing with her horns and made off with a half a sheet. The line was moved to the hillside where cattle did not roam.

In wintertime the washing hung indoors on lines slung between pot hooks on the ceiling. As there was an oil lamp hanging there too this helped the drying process. That persecutor of children's fingers came into use again and the clothes had a final mangle. This meant that the ironing was not quite as demanding.

Irons were heated by the fire – two being heated, one in use. They were usually of different weights and designed for specific tasks. A candle was placed between pieces of cloth and the iron rubbed across it to make the iron run smoother.

To a woman this must have been a long hard day. Clothes were made of heavier textured cloth years ago which took longer to dry and iron. Ironing was very carefully done – even the handerchief corners were precisely matched.'

'My mother-in-law had a flat iron which she heated on the Yorkshire range but not I – a friend who used to live in the lodge at the entrance to Hardwick Hall offered me her paraffin iron. It was cream enamel with a bowl attached to hold the paraffin – this made it very heavy – and another smaller receptacle in which to put the meths, which was then lit and pumped up Tilly-lamp fashion.'

'Washday was a day-long affair. It had usually begun by seven o'clock, and it was no use expecting much dinner. It was cold meat, fried potatoes or bubble and squeak – leftovers from Sunday, eaten with pickles. By the time I came home from school at lunch time (we had two hours' break then, twelve till two) the washing was usually out on the line, methodically hung. My mother had a system. Towels all hung together, socks in pairs hung from the toes, shirts arranged by size and colour, and any garment which was frayed or personal like bras or knickers was hung where no one could see it from next door. Housewives were judged by their washing lines!

Hopefully, the clothes would be dry enough to take in and fold before Mum went off to church to the three o'clock Women's Meeting. On wet days it would mean damp clothes around the house, usually clothes horses around both coal fires, windows steamed up and an unpleasant aroma filling the house. We all dreaded wet Mondays.'

❖ BATH NIGHT ❖

'Bath night was Friday for the three girls and Saturday for the two boys, in a tin bath. The water was boiled by making a fire under the copper in the kitchen, then it was carried in buckets to the living room, to the bath in front of the coal fire. The water had to be emptied by bucket too, then the bath was returned to the hook on the wall in the yard.'

'I grew up in a house where the bath would be lugged out into the kitchen every week. Mum used to save all her ends of soap and put them in the copper to make the water nice for our bath. Each week we had to ladle the water out to empty the bath afterwards.

As a nine year old in 1948 I was invited to stay with a friend who lived close by and I was promised a bath in a proper bathroom. The delight of sitting in that bath, turning on the taps and seeing my legs in clear water stretching out in front of me is as vivid in my memory as if I had experienced it yesterday. And the final joy? I only had to pull out the plug.'

FOOD AND CALLERS TO THE DOOR

Home cured hams, the aroma of baking day, fresh milk brought straight to the door from the churn, shopping days that were as much as social occasions as necessities – keeping a family fed was hard work but there were so many compensations!

KILLING THE PIG

'Memories of pig killing day on our farm in Wardlow are quite vivid, with Fred Gibson from Tideswell coming to do the job, and after the war Fred Furness, a neighbour who had been a butcher in the Forces. Grandma who lived in a cottage down the road would early in the morning light the fire under the big copper boiler and fill it so that we would have plenty of boiling water when required. A galvanised bucket was put in the oven to warm, and the menfolk would go to the pigsty, tie a rope round the pig's snout and with many pushes and shoves get the pig to the building where a trestle table was waiting. Here four men would lift the pig onto the table where it would be shot and its throat cut so that the blood could be caught in the hot bucket. The blood was saved for my mother to make black puddings.

Dad then fetched boiling water to scald the pig so that the hair could be scraped off, using a utensil known as a pig scraper which also had a hook attached for pulling out the pig's cleas (hooves). When scraping was completed a slit was cut out above the hock in each back leg to fit the cambriol (a piece of wood with notches in). A good strong cart rope was then attached and the pig was hoisted up so that it hung from a wooden beam in the

William Bagshaw of Wardlow remembered pig killing day.

roof. Its innards were removed and it was then washed down with clean cold water, a potato put in its mouth, and left for 24 hours so that it would drain and set.

Next day its head was cut off and the carcase cut into two halves, with the leaf fat and pork taken out. Some of the leaf fat was kept for making black puddings and the remainder cut into squares and rendered into lard, with the lard making a residue which was pressed together and eaten as "scraps". The pork was cut into joints and eaten by family and friends who would return the compliment when they killed their pig. Then each half was cut into a side of bacon and a ham, which were left on flat stone benches in the pantry to drain.

A few days later we sprinkled salt on the head and rubbed salt on the rind side of the bacon and hams to make them sweat, also sprinkling brown sugar on the hams. These were then put onto some other stone benches which were dish-shaped so that brine could be collected and ladled back over the bacon and ham. They were left for three to four weeks. The sides were washed well to get the salt off, hung on large hooks from beams in the kitchen to dry and put in muslin bags to keep the flies off and finish curing.

When the bacon or ham was required, large slices were cut off and then sliced into finer slices for cooking. Lovely. The head and tail were used to make brawn; the feet for jelly for pork pies. We also had sausages and ate the liver and heart. The greatest delicacy was the brains. We children had the pig's bladder, blew it up, and used it as a football.'

◈ POACHING AND PIGS ◈

'Life in a country cottage was sometimes idyllic, but often as money was short plenty of poaching went on. Rabbits were poached together with many game birds. One year there was a black rabbit in with the normal brown rabbits. A friend of my father caught this rabbit one night, but he received a good ticking off – it was rather stupid to take the black rabbit as the gamekeeper would notice it was missing and know that someone was poaching.

My father's neighbour kept a few pigs for food. When the time came for the pig to be killed, the blood was kept for making the black pudding. The neighbour came with a bowl and asked my father (a child at the time) to hold it under the pig. The pig was put on to a slab (about table height) and its throat was cut, blood poured out and my father duly held the bowl to catch it. Suddenly the pig got off the slab and ran round the yard, with my father trying to follow with the bowl.'

▨ NO TURNING THE OVEN DOWN ▨

'Baking day was Thursday. One stone of white bread, brown bread, teacakes, pastry, scones and cakes were all baked on the same day, and in that order. There was no turning the oven down when it was hot, so things that needed a hot oven were baked first.'

Getting the milk out in the winter of 1953 at Lower Plumpton.

▣ BREAD, BUTTER AND BEER ▣

'Once or twice a week we had to churn the butter using a hand churn, this took about 20 minutes. Also we had home-baked bread every week, caraway seed cake and swiss buns which were delicious. During the summer we brewed herb beer which was kept in a large earthenware pancheon to be drunk at haymaking time.'

▣ HOT PEAS AND PIES ▣

'Every Friday night in 1935 the call went out: "Hot peas and pies". Basins at the ready, the doors of our terrace houses would open as though on elastic bands. White basins, some with green rings, some with blue rings, some cracked, but all of them immaculately clean were held in the hands of young people like myself eager to sample the delights of the meal to come. Down scoured steps into the street to join the queue that had already formed by the oblong box contraption, the first compartment containing peas, the second meat pies. Underneath the compartments a coke fire glimmered and the aroma of Chanel No 5 was not in the same class. In turn we held out our basins like Oliver Twist for a hot meat pie to be placed in the bottom followed by a ladle of peas. Bliss. The basins were reverently carried across the stone flags, up the steps, through the door to the oilcloth covered table – a meal fit for a king!'

▣ THE DAILY PINT ▣

'In the 1920s, long before the first milk bottle arrived on our doorstep, an elderly, bewhiskered farmer came with his horse and cart to deliver fresh milk from his cows, seven days a week. He brought his large can into the kitchen and holding it between his knees, he poured the milk into his pint measure and then into our basin, set ready on the table. "Top of the milk" in those days was skimmed off the basin with a spoon.

On his rounds the milkman wore an ancient felt hat, and on wet days the rain used to trickle off the brim as he leaned over the milk-can. I remember many times watching anxiously to see if the trickle would land in the milk. It never did.'

'My memories of delivering the daily pinta go back to the 1940s and 1950s when before and after leaving school I helped my father with his milk round. The cows had to be milked, the milk then cooled before we could start. We had a van into which we put the churns of milk and buckets holding two to three gallons with one pint and half pint measures. The milk was carried door to door in the buckets, the customer having jugs ready to pour it into. Sometimes we had to wait while they washed them out. Occasionally children liked to help. Dad would put into a small can what the customer needed and they would deliver it. One boy tried putting a quart into a pint jug – there was milk everwhere on the lady's dresser.

When the regulations came in we could no longer deliver loose milk, it all had to be sent to the dairy. We bought it back in bottles to take to the customers. It cut delivery time as we no longer had to wait for them to answer the door and find a jug.'

'No refrigerators of course, so the milk was kept in the larder on the thrawl, a cold slab, next to the meat safe, a cupboard with a wire mesh door which kept the flies out.'

◙ CALLERS TO THE DOOR ◙

'I lived in a hamlet one mile each way between two villages. We had the muffin man come once a week ringing his bell, with the muffins and crumpets covered over with a green baize cloth. For a great treat we were allowed once to go down to the bakery and see them mixed, shaped and cooked.

Another regular was the hardware man with his horse and cart, smothered in potties of all shapes and sizes, tin baths, forks, spades, shovels, you name it, he'd got it. Inside he carried anything from paraffin to bluebags and pegs. One day a plane frightened his horse, which reared up and overturned the cart – you can imagine the noise!

Best of all was the one-armed ice cream man with his little donkey and cart. He had a board with holes in it to rest the cones in as he filled them with a scoop, a halfpenny or a penny, or sixpence for a basin. We children were fascinated.

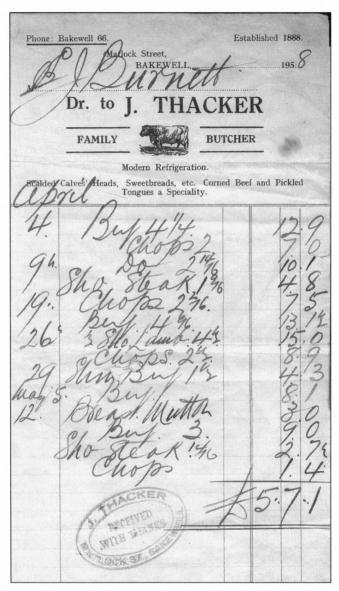

A butcher's bill from 1958.

I also remember Gert and Vi, two buxom sisters with complexions like peaches. They visited all the villages with their fruit and vegetable cart.'

'When I was a small girl, between the two World Wars, most of our household provisions were delivered. The butcher and the grocer had a young whistling lad who came once or twice a week on a bicycle with a large delivery basket on the front. But the baker, milkman, greengrocer, the fishman and "coalie" had a horse and cart and were therefore, to my young mind, much superior to the lad and his bicycle. The last two were my favourites – I wonder why! I would try to sneak out of the house when my mother wasn't looking or if spotted shout a quick, "Just going to feed the horse", and I was away and onto the cart for a forbidden ride to the end of the street where, with a kindly, "Run home now, Missie," Harry or Bill or whatever his name was, would lift me down from the cart. I would then saunter home, putting off my return for as long as possible, for the sequel was always the same – a sound spanking for having run off and got my clothes either coal-dirty or fish-smelly. I never promised not to do it again; it would have been useless. And I'm glad I did, because it is a memory of a carefree bygone age which is now history and a tale to tell the grandchildren.'

'In the 1920s, every Wednesday evening throughout the year, a man delivered paraffin and candles at Alderwasley. He had a horse and covered waggon. On Friday evenings a man walked from Bolehill near Wirksworth; he carried a large basket and sold oatcakes, pikelets and savoury ducks.'

'At Littleover Charlie Whitmore came round – very leisurely – with a horse and dray with vegetables. Freestones, the village grocer, delivered your order and there was great excitement at Christmas. They sent a young man called Victor round with samples of goodies which he displayed on the kitchen table. There were wines, spirits, dates, nuts, crystallised fruits, Turkish delight, and of course, chocolates, sugar pigs and chocolate coins.'

▣ THE LOCAL SHOP ▣

'The village shop was a true Aladdin's cave. A bell clanged when you opened the outside door and a very thick curtain shut off the living quarters. Oh, the lovely smell of candles, paraffin (sixpence a gallon), black lead, donkey stone, moth balls, Shinio, brimstone and treacle and the dreaded syrup of figs! Eight caramels for a penny, bull's-eyes a penny each, aniseed balls six for a penny. A two pound loaf was threepence and a gill of milk a penny ha'penny.'

'After the war goods began to trickle back into the shops and we had more toys and fancy goods to sell, and were able to dress the windows for Christmas. We were often asked to lay things aside for customers who would "fasten" them with a deposit and pay the rest at intervals, usually all coming to collect them on Christmas Eve, when we would be serving all day till eight or nine without a break. Just before Christmas we were honoured by a visit from the local gentry in the form of the Hon Mrs Gell of Hopton Hall on her usual shopping trip to buy small items for the party she gave for the local village children. She did not of course deign to set foot in the shop herself – the Rolls-Royce was drawn up outside (blocking all traffic in St Mary's Gate), and the chauffeur was delegated to go back and forth with a selection of suitably priced items from which she would make her choice. Having done her duty by the lower orders she would then depart without actually having to do any sordid trading. Well, at least we didn't have to salute!'

❖ Going Shopping ❖

'My memory of shopping in Wirksworth goes back to the middle Fifties. My mother would go shopping most days, always early afternoon after doing her main housework. She had a grey pleated skirt which she changed into. We would set off and walk up to the town, sometimes with my Nanna, otherwise just Mum and myself, and always up one side of the road and down the other. I remember certain shops vividly: Slater's butcher's shop, Mrs Mee's just above Lloyds Bank who sold wool and embroidery items etc, where there was always a chair to sit on and a glass topped counter with stock underneath. Next door was Williams ladies' clothing with stock kept in drawers, where they had a full length mirror on legs. The paper shop was next, where I can only remember a very high counter with papers all in order. Next door was Hawley's butcher's where you were served by a very small man in a large white apron, who carried a very large basket. Next I remember the Co-op – haberdashery, furniture, bread and cakes and meat. These shops were all in a row like a mini department store and are no longer with us. We used to go above the haberdashery to view the furniture.

On the other side of the road was Hilton's shoe shop with laces in drawers. Paynes the chemist is still there but is laid out differently. They had very large bottles on the top shelves with blue liquid in them. Mr Read next door sold everything from a pencil to a toy and you could smell the tobacco which he sold loosely and see the toys held behind glass doors. At Bagnalls before self-service everyone wore white overalls and I remember the bacon slicer and shelves stacked high with different foods. Rains butcher's, a small shop. Mrs Maskrey's sweet shop with chocolate behind glass and large bottles of pop where you could choose a flavour and stand in the shop to drink it; there were no cans then.

Mr Cooper the butcher who always used skewers and paper with his name on it, and yours too if you ordered some meat. Mr and Mrs Slater's cycle shop had radios up high on the shelves and cycles in rows and batteries, cigarettes and sweets on the counter. We then walked home and would call at Water Lane Stores where Mum would buy a quarter pound of luncheon meat which was sliced while you waited. Then a long walk down Derby Road.

This seemed to be a ritual every Monday, Thursday and Friday. Tuesday was market day and was different but on the same theme. On all the shopping trips we included talking to lots of people and we always had time for a chat and to enjoy life. Where have all the shops gone? Where has the time gone?'

FROM THE CRADLE TO THE GRAVE

We were much more likely to be born, to suffer illness and to die in our own homes in the past. Home cures were greatly relied on in the days when the doctor charged to visit – but they could not combat those scourges of childhood, scarlet fever and diphtheria.

🔲 PILLS AND POTIONS 🔲

'We always kept a medicine cupboard full of pills and potions. The most used was iodine which was in a green five-sided bottle of rough glass (a warning for those with poor sight that the contents were poisonous). We hated the syrup of figs and it was a good thing we had a double-seater loo because there were five of us and we all had a dose one night a week. Mother used to mix a saucer of butter and sugar for us children to eat when we had a cough, which in memory was much more effective than cough mixtures.'

'Each morning in winter we were given either a dessert-spoonful of cod liver oil and malt or emulsion, supposed to keep us fit. Then Friday night after our baths we all had a teaspoon of brimstone and treacle, to keep our blood "pure".'

'My father had served in the Red Cross in the Great War and cured all injuries with a liberal application of iodine. In my teens I suffered a lot from boils and endured a regular bathing of the affected spot with scalding hot boracic lint. Sometimes my mother would use comfrey as a hot compress, and always swore that it cured my brother's swollen glands which subsided the day before he was due to have an operation to cut them (a common complaint then).'

68

Women's Institutes gave many country women a new social life in the 1920s, here at Coton in the Elms.

◈ IN EMERGENCY ONLY ◈

'In my childhood at Staveley, in the 1920s, the doctor was called in an emergency only. Usually, home-made cures were tried first. For example, we had a comfrey plant and people would come for leaves. It seemed to be a much used remedy. Senna pods, liquorice powder, elderflower tea and goose grease were all used.

If these failed to have the desired effect, you would go to the chemist's shop and buy such things as Bile Beans, Beecham's Pills, Fennings Fever Cure and linseed for those red hot poultices. The one I hated most of all was ipecacuanha wine – an emetic.

As a child I used to have croup and the doctor would come with his dog and stay with me until the attack passed – sometimes quite a few hours. It seems that in those days the GPs had more time for their patients. I was made to wear a chest protector of thermogene in the cold weather and how I detested it! A small piece was pulled off each week and, when spring came, it was just like a piece of string round my neck.

Mother paid sixpence a week to the Nursing Association and this covered hospital treatment but the doctor had to be paid as there was no National Health. He dispensed his own medicines and his fees were well within the reach of our mining community.

It was usually the midwife who brought us into the world but, for our final and ultimate needs, the insurance companies issued penny life policies so that for a penny a week you were sure of a decent funeral.'

✠ INFECTIOUS DISEASES ✠

'Around 1914 to 1915 scarlet fever was rife. Children were taken from Holloway to the Heage fever hospital in black horse-ambulances and they had to stay for about three weeks. Visitors were allowed on Sunday, but parents (mostly mothers as this was

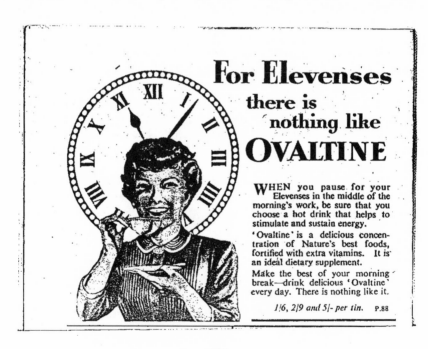

during the war) walked the six or so miles only to see their children at the windows – they were not allowed inside the hospital.'

'In the early 1930s when I was three years old, I became ill with diphtheria and was taken to an isolation hospital a few miles from my home in north-east Derbyshire. It must have been a traumatic experience for me. My parents could only see and talk to me through a window. The only memory I have is of being taken into a room which was full of toys. There, when I went home, I had to leave the doll I had taken in with me. To prevent the spread of infection nothing could be taken away.'

'Early in 1943 just before my twelfth birthday I was ill with yet another sore throat. The doctor was called in once more; he sent for the district nurse, who was quite a forbidding lady, to take a swab of my throat. This was getting to be quite a common occurrence as during the previous year I had similar illnesses and three times was diagnosed to be suffering from German measles. The swab was sent to the Medical Officer of Health in the nearby town and the result this time was positive – scarlet fever. Great consternation – the doctor summoned an ambulance and I was sent to the isolation hospital in Draycott. I had to stay there for six weeks until a negative swab was taken. No visitors were allowed, unless a patient had a parent who was in the Forces and was on leave from abroad and then they *could* visit (perhaps the authorities thought they might take the germ back to the enemy!). My father was determined he was going to check on me, however, so he asked the farmer whose land adjoined the hospital grounds if he could peep over the wall – he did without getting caught.

Back at home the house had to be fumigated with anti-germ smoke and all the doors and windows covered with sheets or blankets to keep the germs in until they had all been "smoked out". Fortunately, the horrid smell had gone by the time I got home.'

◼ A Compensation ◼

'In the early 1930s scarlet fever was a highly serious and infectious disease, requiring quarantine. So I was duly sent to the

Children's Isolation Hospital which was in the countryside, near Belper.

Being so young I can only recall certain memories, one being that visitors could only come rarely (once a week, I believe) by special bus (very few cars in those days). I remember my parents' visits. They were not allowed inside the hospital, so we small patients stood on our beds, with a blanket pinned around us, to look at them through the windows, feeling very wobbly and sad.

For me, a wonderful reward eventually transpired from this illness – I acquired a much longed for doll's pram. While I was in hospital Ripley Fair was under way. This yearly event was one of the highlights of childhood which I would that year, due to the fever, have to forego.

Eventually, after several weeks' isolation, I returned home and to my delight and amazement found, standing in the centre of the living room, magically awaiting my return, the coveted doll's pram. This, at the time, I could not understand. Why was I presented with this much desired gift when it was neither my birthday or Christmas?

I later discovered my father had acquired the pram at the fair. By spending a fortune on the roll-penny and coconut shy he eventually won the wonderful welcome home gift he was determined to get for my homecoming. My mother later told me he had probably spent much more winning this prize at the fair than purchasing it from a store. Of course, it was hugely important to me, for the ones hanging on the fairground stalls were much superior to the shop ones. So, I was compensated both for my illness and missing "The Fair"!'

CHILDHOOD & SCHOOLDAYS

CHILDHOOD DAYS

'An innocent childhood, free to play safely and to explore our surroundings without fear' – whatever the hard times we and our families went through, many of us were fortunate to have a childhood of happy memories.

◈ SOME THINGS YOU NEVER FORGET ◈

'There are some things about childhood which you never forget. I began my schooldays at the age of five in 1916 at Reginald Street school, Derby. My sister and I always wore white starched pinafores and I remember the headmistress who was talking to a mother pointing to me and saying, "That's how I like my children to come to school. That child always looks like that." I ran all the way home to tell my mother what Miss Pickering had said.

When you reached the top class in the infants, if you had been good you were picked to mark rows of crosses in chalk on the hall floor where the children would stand for morning prayers. In the centre of the hall were red and white crosses which were used for maypole dancing. Another little treat was being picked to go round each class and collect the numbers of children present. Back to your own class to add up the numbers and chalk the total on a little board in the hall.

Shrove Tuesday gave us a half holiday and Empire Day (May 24th) was a real treat, with singing in the school yard and someone special coming in to hear us. Lord Roe is the one I remember best. He lived in the big house across from the school.

When I was nine we wore crepe paper bonnets for our Empire Day performance and my teacher, using a safety pin to attach the ribbons, pushed it through the lobe of my ear. I was far too frightened to tell her and went to find my best friend who was much more sensible.

We loved to play in the Arboretum but had to behave. Two

Seven little toy soldiers – dressing up was always fun.

keepers kept us in order. One, "Snappy Jack", walked round with a cane and woe betide anyone stepping over the curved railings round the grass or walking on the hills. Some would dare and if seen Jack would lock the gates until he had given them a good telling off. The other we called "Happy Ambo", he looked after the playground and the swings. The swings were chained to their supports at night and he would start with the small ones and we would run to the next until all were locked away. We played in the street – hide and seek, being careful not to upset the neighbours when we hid in their garden, hopscotch, but only marking the squares where there was a blank wall; and marbles was another favourite until you lost them to your rival.

Money was tight and we couldn't have all we would have liked but my mother and father sacrificed a lot for us. We loved a packet of chips from the local shop and they were wrapped around with newspaper. If we took some papers to the shop they would give us some chips to take home instead of a penny.

Election days were fun. There were two rival committee rooms near us and they each gave the children a coloured ribbon. They would take us for a ride around the streets in a cart and we would sing, "Vote, vote, vote for Mr . . . ." They would drop us off and then we'd run home, change our ribbons and go for another ride singing for the rival candidate.

On Saturday nights my mother and father took us to the market and we would stand fascinated listening to all the traders shouting their prices. They started high but we knew, in the days before refrigeration, prices would fall and people scramble to buy.

Our special treat was to go to the Cosy Cinema on a Saturday afternoon, I think it cost 3d. We had to queue down a long corridor and the best seats were 5d and at the back. We always tried to be at the front of the queue because the seats at the halfway division were always filled first and if you came late you finished on the front row with a crick in your neck from looking up. A very severe man kept order and if there was any noise during a film he would bang on a stool with a wooden stick and shout "Quiet". If the noise continued he would walk to the end of the row, wait to see if the offender did it again and if he did would go along the row, take him from his seat to the door and send him out for the rest of the afternoon.'

❖ The Pit and the Treat ❖

'Born into a mining community at the beginning of the century your life was ruled by "The Pit". When you were 14, if you were male, you automatically went to the pit. If a girl, domestic service. If you came from a large family the girl stayed at home to help mother. If you wed, it was to a village boy or one from the next village. Wherever you went it was the same. Very, very few miners could educate their sons for teaching or other professional work and sadly, in some cases, if they did they found themselves estranged from their son who now spoke differently and was embarrassed by his parents' broad northern accent.

Travel was expensive and buses only just beginning to provide a regular service so entertainment was mainly in the village. The men at the club, their wives with chapel or church work and later they joined the WI when it was formed. A yearly concert played to a packed hall of appreciative miners and their wives.

The manager of the pit was expected at church on Sunday mornings and was usually called upon to read the lesson. The mine owners paid the occasional visit to church when they would be ushered, with great ceremony, to their pew by a garrulous vicar's warden who, later in the vestry, would extol on the munificence of their ten shilling note laid like a blanket on the pile of threepenny bits.

Once a year a "treat" was laid on at Rowthorne for the schoolchildren. This usually took place on a very hot day in August when a high hay cart came to collect the youngest children who were piled into the cart like so many sheep. You learned to grab a side to hang on to and made sure you were not next to the kid who was always sick. We lurched and screamed as we bumped over the uneven road, pulled by a single horse, up the hill. The older children had to walk beside us with the harassed teachers who had to cope with the inevitable request of "Miss, I want to go", and boys, uneasy in best clothes, bent on various nefarious escapades.

The headmistress awaited us at the top of the hill – having taken the bus. She was built like an Amazon warrior, a Queen Mary vogue hat on her head and a furled umbrella under her arm, and had a look that could kill at 20 paces. She would inspect us all, with our sweaty faces and limp hair ribbons, tell us all in scathing tones what we were and what we looked like, then turn around and lead us, a bedraggled army, to the Hall.

When we arrived, "They" awaited us and with a lot of gushing and showing of teeth we were ushered into the stable yard where trestle tables were laid out with sandwiches, curled by the heat, and large brown jars of home-made jam – rhubarb and fig. The wasps had a field day. They got the jam and us. At the end of the "eat up your crusts" instruction, the plate of cakes was brought round. When asked to choose the one you liked it was promptly cut in two! This led to a lot of muttering, especially if you had your eye on the cream horn and the kid next to you wanted the chocolate bun.

After a drink of diluted orange we had an educational tour of the gardens which largely fell on deaf ears. Games followed and nuts were thrown for us to scramble for. I fear I was an ungracious child. When one of the sons gave me a push to go, I said, rudely, that I didn't like nuts! At the end of the day we lined up for a bag of boiled sweets which were always the same. Fishes, pink one side, yellow the other, and an indigestible Bath bun boiled in oil and rolled in sugar. We licked the sugar off and used them for footballs and snowballs as we went home down the hill. Home, to the never to be forgotten smell of home-made bread just out of the oven. Golden, crispy loaves, that today are as far away as the Annual Treat.'

▨ IN THE ORPHANAGE ▨

'My life during the 1920s and 1930s in Old Glossop began on the 4th July 1923, as the eldest child of an accountant employed at the old LMS Railway – but unfortunately my father died on the 3rd November 1930 from tuberculosis contracted in the trenches in the First World War. He was just 37 years old.

In March 1931 my mother made me a resident of the Railway Servants' Orphanage, Ashbourne Road, Derby (after the war known as St Christopher's). I was later joined by my brother Walter (four years younger) who was fostered until he was old enough to come to the orphanage. I left in July 1938.

I went to Ashbourne Road school and then to Kedleston Road school until I was 14 years old – for the next year I was kept at "home" and taught every aspect of housework. It was very rough and hard, scrubbing floors, cleaning toilets, washing and ironing in the laundry – oh, it was so old fashioned, "real Victorian", but the best was when it was my turn to go to the kitchen to help – we got all sorts of titbits.

Our meals consisted of: Sunday – roast meat, potatoes and veg; Monday – stew; Tuesday – liver and bacon with potatoes and veg; Wednesday – roast meat, potatoes and veg; Thursday – stew; Friday – fish, parsley sauce and potatoes; Saturday – corned beef, potatoes and pickles. We always had a pudding. We had boiled eggs twice a week for breakfast and porridge – or

Walter and his sister, who grew up in the Railway Servants' Orphanage at Derby in the 1930s.

bread and jam. Tea was always bread and jam plus cake twice a week.

Our leisure time in the evenings was taken up by several activities. Sunday we had an evening service (in the home although we had been to Sunday school in the morning and afternoon and church in the morning to St John's church). Monday was choir practice. On Tuesday there was a mid week service, and on Wednesday gym. The gym was very well equipped and in 1938 I won the cup for the best all round athlete of the year. Thursday was Guides. I was patrol leader for the Chaffinch Patrol. We had our own Guide Company. Our Captain was one of our officers and our Lieutenant was Lady Fitzherbert Wright of Kedleston Hall and such a lovely lady she was. On Friday, when old enough, we had to repair our own clothes. Saturday we had a film show (or should I say "lantern slides", even so we enjoyed them).

It was a very Victorian and austere upbringing but we were well fed, clothed and kept warm. We had a matron and our carers were called officers and maids. Our clothing consisted of gym slips, navy blue jumpers, cream blouses for Sundays, black woolly stockings and boots – shoes on Sunday. We had floral dresses for the summer and cream ankle socks which we knitted for ourselves; I am still addicted to knitting.

At Christmas we would hang up our stockings and always there was a new penny, an apple, orange and sweets. Friends of the home came and served us at our tables. We were truly kings and queens for the day and in the evening we had people come and entertain us and afterwards they would give each child a box of chocolates (oh, such bliss).

The orphanage was kept open by the ordinary workers of the combined railway companies. The children whose parent contributed got preference for a place. My father had contributed the one penny which was the normal fee. I later paid a contribution as I worked for British Rail from 1940 to 1976 so I like to think I said a very humble "thank you" to the Railway for my upbringing in the home. It was a very strict regime but in hindsight that was necessary with so many children under one roof. (I would not have said that 60 years ago!)'

❖ A Pair of Shorts ❖

'At Littleover in the early 1930s we had fields to play in stretching from Constable Drive to Chain Lane, where I can remember my dog chasing hares. How many remember the common that ran from Crich Avenue to Uttoxeter Road where the City Hospital now stands? It was a wonderful place for us children to climb trees, make dens, and in the winter go tobogganing. I was always getting into trouble for going home with a torn dress. Alas, my mother wouldn't let me wear shorts. Little girls didn't, in those days. However, I think my father had always wanted a son and it wasn't too difficult to get round him. One Saturday I arranged to meet him secretly on his way home from work. We went into Derby and he took me into the Midland Drapery and bought me a pair of shorts and a T-shirt. The shop assistant seemed quite amused. I was so thrilled with my shorts.

Traffic was increasing in 1948 but London Road, Derby still presented no problems for a young boy on his own.

I don't think my mother was too upset as she didn't have any more dresses to mend – and how much easier it was to climb those trees!'

▣ GROWING UP IN THE 1930S ▣

'Smells have a very nostalgic place in my memory. The smell of fruit and it must be Christmas, as I'm sure that was the only time the fruit bowl on our dresser was full, fruit being a luxury in those days. When I had to dry my babies' nappies around the fire I was transported back to that steamy living kitchen, on wet Mondays, clothes all around the fire, the white-topped table still damp after Mam had scrubbed the clothes on it. When we had to have dinner Mam would put the clean Sunday newspapers on instead of a tablecloth, and dinner was always mutton stew with lentils, followed by rice pudding; both of these had been simmering all morning in the fire oven, and didn't they taste good. Mam's rice pudding always had the best nutmegged skin in all the world, or so I said as I was allowed to scrape the dish out.

When I was about four years old I had measles complicated by pneumonia, and I lay feeling so poorly on a hard leather sofa that wouldn't have given an inch if hit with a hammer, let alone with the weight of a sick child. My bed was brought down, and I watched in amazement as Dad carried a shovel of coals from the range in the kitchen and put them in the grate in the parlour where I was to be nursed. While I watched Dad making up this fire in the most sacrosanct of rooms, I really thought I must be dying. You see, we lived in a very small two-bedroomed terraced town house and the parlour was only ever used on special occasions, like when it had to double as a sick room, and also at Christmas time. The delight of roasting chestnuts on the open fire, and cracking nuts with the flat iron on the hearth, and the smell of burning orange peel brings all this back to me.

One Christmas I got some woollen gloves in my stocking, they actually had fingers. I'd never had "proper" gloves before, and when it snowed I made do with an old well darned pair of Dad's socks, with a piece of elastic at the wrist. I went after dinner to visit a great-aunt with Dad, and she gave me a threepenny "dodger" (I thought she must be very rich). On the way home I dropped it in the street, and couldn't pick it up with my new gloves on. No way was I taking them off. I think Dad must have picked it up for me.

Do you remember some of the humiliations you suffered as a child, and wondering if your Mam really loved you if she let these things happen to you? One I remember very clearly. I was always "chesty" in the winter, and Mam used to knit me woollen vests in a special fisherman's yarn called Ab wool; it still retained the lanolin even after several washes, but it became a lovely soft cream texture. The reason I hated them was that Mam always put in elbow-length sleeves, and I dreaded the warmer weather coming, because I was always put in dresses before I was allowed to cast my vest, and it was so difficult trying to keep my vest sleeves rolled up under my dress sleeves. The other horror was having to wear navy blue knickers, as the elastic in one leg always went at the worst possible moment, and would hang down below my gym slip.

Do you remember being able to buy a ha'p'orth of goody waste from the corner shop? All the boiled sweets had been bashed about when they were being weighed, so there was a sugary residue in the bottom. The canny shopkeepers of the Thirties put the waste in sweet bags, and sold it for a halfpenny. You'd just lick your finger and dip it in the bag, and then suck your finger clean. It was delicious, all the fruit tastes mingling together, and sometimes if you were really lucky you'd find small pieces of actual sweet.'

❖ In Trouble ❖

'I used to live in St John Street, Clifton and spent a very happy time there with friends and neighbours. We spent some of the time in our warehouse playing on the hoist which was used for hauling up the sacks of corn from the street.

In the garden with my energetic friends we played games, follow my leader, rounders, and climbing trees which were at the bottom of the garden, some of the branches spread over the river Henmore. I was swinging on a branch one day when it broke and

83

I fell about twelve feet into the water. Luckily I did not suffer, but was a bit wet.

We overlooked Shawcroft where we used to enjoy the fairs arriving and the circus; the elephants and horses were washed and brushed down in the Henmore. The menageries used to stay on the Market Place, all caged up. I had a ride on an elephant. I was the last to be lifted on and I seemed very near to the tail wafting about. We had to hold on to the child in front. I was frightened of falling off, and then we paraded around the Market Place.

My friends and I used to play in Bradley Wood where I fell into a bog up to my waist. Joan and Joyce found two small branches and got me to hold each one and helped me out. They took my clothes off and put their blazers around me. There was quite a gang of us and they ran around trying to dry my clothes. I told them not to tell my parents but a day or two later my mother bumped into Mrs Spencer and was asked how I was. She was taken aback and asked why? Mrs Spencer said that Joan had had a nightmare, shouting "Get Mary out". All was revealed.

Another day I thought that my auntie's dog would like a swing on the recreation ground. I put him in a swing which had bars on three sides, and I put his lead across the front, and when I pushed him he slid and nearly fell out, though the lead saved him. I did not tell my aunt, but when I went some time later to take him out, he crept underneath their sideboard and wouldn't come out, and she asked me what I had done to him.

We used to celebrate most things in the house or garden, such as making a maypole. Mrs Pearson was very good at this, she had two round hoops and put them together and we had ribbons on them and paraded to their house and ours.

When we found a dead bird we used to have a funeral, putting the bird in a box and covering it up with leaves and one of us would be the vicar and we had a little service and sang a hymn or two.'

🔹 FORTUNATE CHILDREN 🔹

'I was an only child but never a lonely child. My best friend was one of a large family and I was treated as an honorary member, enjoying the rough and tumble of a family group.

At Betteridge Stables, Repton in 1946.

The highlight of our week was the Saturday morning penny filmshow, where we joined others in cheering the cowboy hero and booing the villain. We would sit on the edges of our seats watching Rin Tin Tin (the Wonder Dog) in his adventures.

There were no expensive toys – money was tight but we made our own entertainment. In the winter evenings we would wait for Johnny the Lamplighter to come round on his cycle to light the street gas lamps with his long pole, then warmly wrapped, we would play our games under the lights, possibly queueing to take turns to ride someone's scooter. Going home, glowing, and most likely with chapped knees, we would get the Snowfire treatment. Can anyone remember that hard, green block which turned chapped legs to fire and made you hop? After the initial torture it actually worked.

On the school summer holidays we took our jam sandwiches and bottle of water and went off after breakfast for a picnic (unaccompanied by adults). We would play, roll down the grassy slopes, paddle in the brook and return home in time for tea.

The cynics will no doubt say that looking back, life only seemed to be rosier. I say they are wrong. We certainly did not have the material excess of today's children, but we were allowed to have an innocent childhood and do childish things, free to play safely and explore our surroundings without fear. We were, indeed, very fortunate.'

GAMES AND TREATS

Our games were seasonal and our playground usually the road, with little equipment to buy. There were rules for all our games, which we obeyed without question though it is hard to know who actually told us what they were! The Saturday treat was often a visit to the cinema, or to the sweetshop with our pocket money penny.

▦ THE GAMES WE PLAYED ▦

The house at Staveley where I was born in the 1920s was a two-up and two-down in a row of six houses. At the back was a communal yard that made an excellent playground for us and our friends.

Our toys were simple and seemed to have their season. Around Shrove Tuesday, out would come whips and tops for the boys, shuttlecock and battledore for the girls. Then there might be a craze for hidey or skipping to be followed quickly by marbles, "fag-card" skimming or hopscotch.

If it was windy we made crude kites with newspaper and ran with them up and down the yard doing our utmost to get them to fly. We were rarely successful but it never seemed to dampen our ardour. Sometimes we rolled hoops which were just rough pieces of wood from the butter barrels. We were always inventive and made our own versions of the endless ball games.

Our own particular game in the yard was one which we made up and called "traffic jams". It consisted of racing madly round the yard on anything which had wheels, such as our scooters, little wooden tricycles, boxes on wheels (made by versatile fathers who kept a keen look-out for likely materials – nothing was wasted in those days), even old push-chairs were pressed into use and would be scooted along with the other vehicles.

We were very lucky, for at one end of our yard was the

communal washhouse that had a room above it that had probably been some kind of storage place. In wet weather we took to the "top place" and prepared our concert. After days and days of very serious rehearsal, we would invite our parents to the performance, for which privilege they had to pay a halfpenny each. They were always appreciative of our efforts and would say that they had paid good money to see much worse on the real stage.'

'The way to Kirk Hallam school was down the hill, underneath the railway bridge, pausing to shout to the guard of the passing goods train going to Stanton ironworks: "Jack in the box, Jack in the box, give me a penny for washing your pots." This was obligatory, we all did it.

At night I remember playing around the gas lamp by our home at Little Hallam – hopscotch, kick tin lurky, whip and top, battledore and shuttlecock, and skipping using the plaited rope which arrived round the crates of oranges sold for pancake day.'

'I was born in 1921 in a house in the old Pot Market in Tideswell. Four or five of us children lived in the Pot Market so I

We had fun with simple toys.

had plenty of friends to play with – hopscotch and marbles, bowling a hoop or skipping. We played out there in the hours after school when we had done our chores. One final treat we all looked forward to and hated to miss. The old man who had a fruit shop next door to our house kept his horse stabled in the Manchester Road and we looked forward to climbing onto his cart each evening for the ride. He was the lamplighter too, and went along the streets with his hooked pole to pull down the chain which lit each lamp.

When it got too dark outside we played dominoes or tiddlywinks which weren't too noisy, while Mum knitted or sewed and Dad, who had to abandon his spade when the light went, walked off for a game of darts or a pint.'

'In the 1950s we "played out" with skipping ropes with wooden handles and ballbearings, scooters, trikes and cycles. Trikes had a long pole attached for the parents to hold and a "boot" sloping down between the two rear wheels, a brake and a bell – the louder the better. Our scooters had a wooden step centre and a large metal brake at the back.'

❖ SATURDAY TREAT ❖

'On Saturday afternoons in the 1920s my mother gave me threepence. Our village hall at Youlgreave was then a YMCA and a cinema on Saturday, so it was twopence to go in to see the comedy film in the afternoon and the other penny was to spend at a local shop on sweets. A large stove warmed the hall and you

Acting in the Baslow pantomine was a real treat for local children.

could take chestnuts to cook while you watched a silent picture accompanied by a Mrs Rose on the piano.'

'In the 1950s Saturday was special at Woolworths, with its maroon and cream glossy decor and crowned "W". To buy a chicken cob and a milk shake was really something, not readily available elsewhere as it would be today.'

▣ ON THE WAY TO SCHOOL ▣

'On the way to school if we were lucky enough to have a halfpenny to spend, we had a wide choice of sweets or goodies to choose from. Tiger nuts were an ugly wrinkled nut which tasted very sweet, and there were liquorice wood which was chewed until it hung in shreds, aniseed balls and Cadbury's halfpenny bars of chocolate.'

SCHOOLDAYS: THE BEST
YEARS OF OUR LIVES?

Long walks to school, cold Victorian classrooms, wet clothes steaming round the stove, strict discipline – just some of the memories of schooldays up to the 1950s. Village schools changed very little over the generations, but many of us have cause to thank the dedication of those hardworking teachers.

▣ COMBS SCHOOL IN 1915 ▣

'I was born at Combs on Christmas Day 1910 and spent all my childhood and teenage years on the family farm. At the age of five I walked daily with my ten year old sister to the village school which was also the Primitive Methodist chapel. There were no more than 18 children attending.

There was no playground so we had to play on the road. At the side was a ditch which we used to jump and if we got our feet wet, we were in trouble. We played tick but not many ball games as the neighbours complained because the ball went into the meadows.

The vestry was the cloakroom with pegs at the back to hang our coats on. There was a small fireplace and a brown clay pot sink with only a cold water tap. Attached to the building were two lean-to buildings containing pan toilets, one for the girls and one for the boys. In the one classroom there was a balcony on which stood the pulpit. We were never allowed up there, nor were we to touch the bible. The school was heated by a big iron stove which we sat round in cold weather, and lit by pretty brass paraffin lamps hung from the ceiling.

We went home for dinner except when the weather was bad when we took sandwiches (home-made bread, butter and jam) with the teacher making us cocoa on the stove. I recall the children from Greave House bringing black treacle butties.

The headteacher was Mrs Coates. She was a good looking lady with grey hair, not afraid of using the cane, and always went very red when visitors or inspectors came in. We respected her greatly. To get to school she travelled daily from Buxton to Chapel-en-le-Frith South station, then walked in all weathers the two miles to school, always there at 9 am. I remember pupil teachers Florence Morten and Daisy Shirt, whose mother was the caretaker.

The day began with prayers, a hymn and a scripture lesson, then the three Rs. In the afternoon we had geography, needlework and history. We sat at long desks with slots in which to place the slates which we wrote on and cleaned with a damp cloth. Later we graduated to pencil, then pen and ink. The pens were wooden holders with a metal end into which was inserted a nib, which had to be changed regularly. The inkwell was in the right-hand corner of the desk and blotting paper was essential. A familiar sound heard every day was us all chanting, in sing-song voices, multiplication tables. I recall having to write lines, "I must not talk in class".

How we all hated the "Nit Nurse", Miss Major, coming and rifling through our hair. The medical officer Dr Hannan used to come on horseback and always tied his horse to the gatepost. I remember Billy Lomas, the coalman, coming with his horse and lorry. He used to look through the windows and pull faces at us, making us laugh.

The clothes I remember wearing were a plaid coat made by a deaf and dumb lady, Miss Storer of Chapel, which lasted me ten years (clothes were made to grow into); a hand-knitted woollen hat (which I made at school); gloves; woollen vest and jumper or blouse; liberty bodice; flannel knickers and petticoat; serge skirt and always a white pinafore. My black stockings (brown for Sundays) were well darned and held up by garters. The boys wore clogs and girls black button boots which were suitable for rough walking as the majority lived at outlying farms. In 1920 pupils were provided with rope-soled canvas slippers to wear in school. I think I left school when I was nearly 14. Most of the boys went into farming and the girls stayed at home as I did, or went into domestic service.'

▣ PLEASANT NOSTALGIA ▣

'It is with pleasant nostalgia I recall my childhood in Burbage in the 1920s – the village school, now empty and derelict; the headmaster affectionately known as "Chips"; Miss Nivens, who kept toffees in her cupboard, a reward for work well done. There were a number of pupils who lived a distance away, who went home for lunch (no school meals then) and returned for the afternoon lessons. The kindly caretaker dried their clothes on wet days and gave them hot drinks. Then there was "Daddy Hall", the attendance visitor who called at your home to see if you were really indisposed or playing truant. We looked forward to the Christmas party with presents from the tree and felt very sophisticated carrying our cards with our partner's name and dancing. In the summer there were school sports, picnics, tennis and cricket matches to watch; the grounds have long gone, taken over for building.'

▣ EMPIRE DAY ▣

'I started at Youlgreave school in 1922 and remember Empire Day, 24th May, and how patriotic it was. Every child was given a daisy and told that it represented the Empire. The petals were the countries of the Empire and the centre was us.

On Fridays everyone took their own duster and polish to do their desk, and how exciting it was when the top class had new desks that opened! After school a favourite place to visit was the blacksmith. Besides the horse being shod, and iron bands made for the cart wheels, if he wasn't too busy he would make iron bowling hoops for the boys to play with.'

▣ DISCIPLINE FROM EARLY DAYS ▣

'I remember starting school at Beighton at five years old. Mother took me for the first day or two – after that we set off with our small friends. This was at the beginning of the 1930s. We had hot malted milk in the morning break. We went home for lunch which meant we made the journey to and from school four times a day – almost a mile each time. There wasn't much traffic on the roads so it was quite safe and there was always a friendly "bobby" on the beat but despite his friendliness we children steered quite clear of him whether we had been naughty or not.

We were shown discipline right from the early years. We dare not move from our desks without permission and had to put up our hand if we wished to speak or "leave the room". We were taught about history and patriotism – we always had a little play on Empire Day (24th May) and the National Anthem was one of the first songs we learned together with *All things bright and beautiful* and *Gentle Jesus* – the latter being the prayer most children said before they climbed into bed, together with the Lord's Prayer.

Into junior school where we learned to write "properly" and we prepared to "sit for the scholarship" – it was quite an achievement to pass.

Off to secondary school, having passed! Stiffer discipline there; although it was a mixed school we were not allowed to mix with the boys outside class time (although we did try). If we were reported by the public for misbehaving on the school bus or out in public we were severely reprimanded by the Head.'

◘ PART OF THE FUN ◘

'My family came to Breadsall in 1934 and the next year I started school. Everyone walked to school through the fields using the footpaths. There were no cars to transport us there. The older children looked after the younger ones and there was a sense of caring for each other. In fact, part of the fun of going to school was the walking there and back. There were no school dinners so we all walked home at lunchtime, even children who lived a considerable distance away.

Breadsall being a Church of England school, we had prayers and religious instruction every morning. The Catechism was learned by heart, as were the psalms. The school building dated from 1837 and consisted of three classrooms. There was no central heating, just a large open fire with a metal guard round on which we hung our gloves after playing in the winter snow. Children attended the school until they were 14 and then left to

Children from Overdale school, Littleover in the 1930s.

go to work, unless you passed the scholarship at eleven to attend the grammar school in Derby.'

❖ WRITING IN SAND ❖
'My first school in Willington in the 1930s was with Miss Keeling in a private house. When I started aged three and a half we had sand trays (about the size of a Swiss roll tin) full of fine sand. You traced your letters with your forefinger, then shook the tray and it disappeared. This was how you learned.'

❖ FOUNDER'S DAY ❖
'I started at Wirksworth infants' school in 1926 at the usual age of five, and remember best being set with the rest of the class to knit dishcloths from soft string – and the trouble I had with them. I don't think I ever finished one in all my time there.

At the age of eleven I gained a scholarship to Wirksworth grammar school and, attired in the school uniform of navy and gold, began the next and happiest stage of my education. I can, however, recall very few highlights, the main one being the annual Founder's Day, when the whole school travelled to Hopton Hall, the home of the Hon Mrs Gell, descendant of the founder and a great character in her own right.

Before partaking of the tea provided there was a price to pay – namely massing before the main steps to be addressed by the honourable lady in person, resplendent in black bombazine and jet set off by a remarkable bonnet. A considerable author (in her own estimation), having written the school song among other items, she lectured us at length in true Victorian fashion on fighting for the Empire and doing our duty to those in authority, ending with a poem from her own pen. After inspiring us with these thoughts she retired and we were free after tea to roam the grounds and hunt for toads in the undergrowth. I also remember an ancient set of stool-ball bats which must have mouldered away long ago. Hopton Hall is no longer the home of the Gell family, it was sold a few years ago, but I still see it across the Carsington Water sometimes, and remember.'

◈ LITTLE EATON IN THE 1940S ◈

'We went to the local school in Little Eaton three quarters of a mile away from home, walking there and back and coming home for dinner. My ambition in the infants' class was to play triangle in the band. The boys played the drums, and the girls shook tambourines vigorously as "Wee Willie Winkie" ran down the stairs, but a favoured few tinkled the triangles. I never realized my ambition!

As we moved up the school, work became harder and the dreaded eleven-plus exam loomed large. My best friend and I were thrilled to be awarded places at the girls' grammar school in Derby and one of the boys also passed for Bemrose School. This was a record, as in previous years only one scholarship had been awarded each year, alternately to a boy and then to a girl. There were more places available to the town schools and it was very difficult for country children to get a good secondary education.

We always looked forward to 24th May which was the anniversary of Queen Victoria's birthday and Empire Day. The partitions between the classrooms were removed and the whole school joined together to sing patriotic songs, *Here's a Health unto His Majesty*, *The British Grenadiers* and so on. This was followed by a half day's holiday.

Sports Day was another highlight of the year and particularly the fancy dress competition. We were lucky to have a magnificent cowboy outfit which won prizes for members of the family in turn, but other competitors showed much more imagination. During the war one family dressed their children up in blackout material covered with empty cigarette packets and labelled themselves "Fagged Out". Fortunately for us the war hardly impinged on our young lives. My most vivid memories are of the smell of the gas masks we carried, and the endless stream of army lorries in convoy as they drove along the main road past our school. We used to dash out and wave to the soldiers who grinned and waved back in answer.'

▣ I REMEMBER THE FOOD ▣

'Bemrose School, Derby, before the war was largely a fee-paying school, with over 600 pupils. A cooked meal was provided for the sum of 3s 6d per head per week. It was a source of joy to all diners when, at the outbreak of war, the refectory was turned into a large ARP post and we all had to either cycle home or take sandwiches. The pre-war standard of food was appalling and has left memories of liver, tripe and onions, semolina, and tapioca pudding, which was known as "frogspawn".'

▣ CLIFTON SCHOOL 1938–1942 ▣

'Walking from Town End over the wooden bridge which spanned the little stream by Chapel Cottage, following the footpath through the golf links to the stile near the school where we congregated in the school yard until the whistle sounded, we all lined up in our appropriate classes quietly and filed into the classroom. Miss Lilian Bold, headmistress, came from

Ashbourne in her car which she garaged for the day at the vicarage, the building now gone; she taught the older children.

Miss Mary Stewart, the infants' teacher, lived at Trellis Cottage. She played the piano for morning assembly, a hymn and prayers every morning. The vicar, Reverend Claude Ambrose Perkins, visited the school several times a week to take assembly; the church was very much part of the school and many of the children were in the choir. We were taught scripture and the three Rs every day by Miss Stewart and each afternoon she would read us a story from Enid Blyton's *Sunny Stories*, something we all looked forward to as we knew afterwards it was prayers and hometime.

The school doctor visited occasionally, when everyone was thoroughly checked, weighed and measured, teeth checked also, and sometimes a visit had to be arranged to the Stone House, Ashbourne now St Oswald's Hospital, where the school dentist did fillings and extractions, usually with gas after which you came round on a mattress laid on a black iron bedstead. Despite this the thought of walking down Church Bank to the station and returning by train soon lifted your spirits.

In winter the school was quite warm with radiators heated by the coke boiler. Nevertheless, in extreme weather a fire was lit in the main room, which was divided from the infants' area by a wooden screen which rolled up when necessary, and we were given hot Horlicks instead of milk at morning break.

During the war gas masks were taken to school and there was air raid practice, causing much excitement amongst the children. No school meals so village children returned home for lunch whilst those from Snelston and Collycroft brought sandwiches.

Fondest memories are of nature walks taken at all seasons, to Sprinks Wood, Dobbin Lane, Paradise, Green Lane and over the golf links collecting wild flowers, studying the trees and the countryside. Games were played, rounders, stool ball, skipping and dancing, and singing lessons with Miss Stewart. It was a happy environment and I am pleased it is still thriving successfully today.'

❖ OFF TO AMBER VALLEY CAMP ❖

'By 1947 the war had been over for two years and the sense of anti-climax had produced a stilted, boring school life. So it was with growing interest that we heard the headmistress announce that we could go for two months to Amber Valley Camp school. At that time there were no school holidays abroad and so the thought of two whole months away from Wellington Street girls' school, Long Eaton and Miss Parker's strict eagle eye, albeit we would still have lessons, seemed too good to be true and I and five other girls "signed up" to go. It would cost ten shillings a week and we were to take our ration books. Parents could visit every other Sunday.

On 12th April we set off on a hired local bus and one hour later we arrived at Amber Valley Camp school (now Ogston Reservoir). I can still feel the excitement on seeing four large and two small wooden chalets. These were three for the girls and three for the boys, 50 children in the large and 20 in the small, making 120 boys and 120 girls. Each chalet dormitory had a Derbyshire name, eg Wingfield or Eyam. Each chalet had one

Amber Valley Camp gave children a welcome break from school routine after the war.

99

teacher. We slept in two-tier bunk beds and every morning around 7 am we went for a wash in the "ablutions block". What a wonderfully exciting time that two months was. Many lessons were taken outdoors, eg painting, some of us sitting in the middle of a stream on boulders. A small light engine we called Peggy which hauled stone past the camp became part of our day. Meals were taken in another large wooden hut. And could we eat! We cleared the post office at Woolley Moor of everything edible and every day a fruit van would appear, when we would buy sixpence worth of apples, grapes etc. We were fed very well but the outdoor life made us so hungry. We had dances, sports, and unusual lessons such as bee keeping and poultry keeping as well as surveying.

There is so much about life there I could tell you. Suffice it to say, they were two of the happiest months of my whole school life.'

◙ NOT A GOOD START ◙

'My schooldays began in the mid 1950s at Wingerworth, when my best friend Linda and I held hands and sat quivering in our seats as the teacher wrenched a screaming child from its mother's arms. Then, parents were definitely not encouraged to ease their children through the first days of school! Our seat of learning was a Victorian building – the windows began at five feet off the ground so there was no chance of looking outside and daydreaming, and the heating consisted of a pipe that ran along the walls. Apart from warming up cold hands and feet, it was very useful when small bottles of milk needed defrosting at mid morning break.'

◙ LONGFORD IN THE 1950S ◙

'Our schoolroom had high windows and a large fireplace that held a warming fire in winter. The frozen milk would be brought in, in its crates, and stacked in front of the fire to thaw. Gloves would be put on the guard after snowballing or building snowmen in the playground. Mrs Turner was the infants' teacher and taught us how to add up and take away by drawing cats and rabbits. If visitors came, out came our sand trays and sticks to keep us quiet.

While I was at the school a kitchen was built on the back, over the boys' playground. Until then we had to walk up the road to the Pump House every day, whatever the weather. The dinners were cooked in there so it was warm and welcoming. Then in the playground climbing frames appeared; one of them had a scramble net on that seemed ever so high for a short while. Up until then all we had to play with was the coke pile for the stove.'

❖ BRETBY SCHOOL ❖

'The school in the late 1950s had a very large playing field and what fun we had, our own Cresta Run on those cold snowy days when we all took our sledges to school and raced down the slippery slope. Then there was sports day in the summer with

Hilton school open day in 1965.

101

the mums and other family members attending, and the obstacle race where amongst other things we had to eat a jam doughnut hanging on a piece of string with our hands behind our backs and struggle under that old tarpaulin of my father's that had all those sheep sheared on it a few weeks before.

We started practising for the Christmas play in October (after half term); everyone had a part from the youngest child and our costumes were all painstakingly made out of crepe paper. After the performance there was the Christmas party to look forward to with a visit from Father Christmas who had a present for each child.

After Mrs Spencer, the infants' teacher, left to have her first baby all of us (about 20 to 25) were taught in the same classroom by Miss Hindson and she coped with us all and many of us managed to pass our eleven-plus to the local grammar school.

Miss Hindson let the older ones make her morning coffee (Camp) in the school kitchen. Dinners were delivered every day in containers from Swadlincote and Mrs Worthington, our dinner lady, served them up. We were also allowed to cook small cakes in Miss Hindson's kitchen, of course under supervision, another treat.

The school never had "proper" toilets and we never seemed to mind the run across the yard even in the bad weather, but I can still remember the smell when the men came to empty the toilets each week.

The village had no other meeting place so the school was used for many activities. The WI met there and had their own pot cupboard in the little room. There were whist drives held regularly during the winter months and the parish council met there too. The annual Sale of Work for the church just at the top of the green was held in the school. The school was the distribution centre for the orange juice and cod liver oil for the younger children and of course we took our "savings money" each Monday to buy savings stamps.'

THE WORLD OF WORK

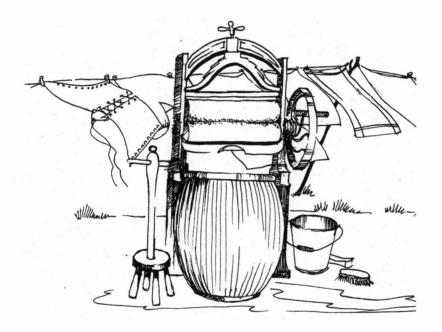

ON THE LAND

Life on the land hardly seemed to have changed since Victorian times, with horses supplying the power on the farms until at least the 1940s and hiring fairs still providing a place for farmer and labourer to meet. "Hard work and not much money" – that was the experience of many families, but there were good memories too.

◙ ON MY GRANDPARENTS' FARM ◙

'I spent holidays at my Grandma's in the 1920s. She lived on a farm up Axe Edge. The water was fetched from a well in two buckets, ladled with a lading can. It was very good water, especially when it was frosty. Everything was cooked on an open fire with hooks to hang the kettles on. The lamps were lit at dusk and put on the table to read by until bedtime. Then my Gran wrapped up an oven shelf in a flannel bag to warm the bed and we sank into feathers for the night.

Haymaking was special. My uncle got up early and mowed with a scythe, then the grass was turned by hand until it was dry. Two wooden poles were then laid on the field and the hay was loaded on top and carried down the steep hillside to the barn. This was called "stanging". The first good sheaf was tied and sent to the church for harvest.'

◙ HORSES AND HIRING ◙

'One pleasant memory of my village childhood in the late 1930s and early 1940s was of the shire stallions that walked through Biggin on Saturday evenings. They were truly magnificent animals, always groomed to a satin-like sheen and their tails and manes plaited with red, gold, blue and green ribbons.

The two I remember were Spitfire and Wenlock Peony belonging to Mr John Etches of Roystone Grange near Parwich.

Horsepower in action at Home Farm, Rowsley.

They were led by a small man with a London accent which was a novelty to us children, we being used to broad Derbyshire accents.

As my father was the local farrier blacksmith, the horse was led up our garden path and the two men would have a "sup of tea and a puff o' bacca" while they discussed the horse's feet, but really to talk about any gossip that had been picked up on the week's walk round the neighbouring villages. Before the advent of television and mass media coverage, anyone who had been on the road visiting other villages was always very welcome with all the bits of news he had gathered.

With the change in breeding methods, stallions are no longer walked round the farms and are just a pleasant memory of my childhood.

Until the early 1930s, a large fair was always held on land near the Newhaven Hotel – that is about halfway between Ashbourne and Buxton on the A515.

It was a pleasure fair with boxing booths, fire-eaters, jugglers and pedlars etc, but it was also a hiring fair where people went hoping to find a worker to be hired.

My father often told me how as an eleven year old (around 1906), he was taken to the fair by his father and hired as farm servant for one year. His wage would be £1 5s for the year with one half day off per month. He had to be in by 9 pm from his half day off and he told of the night he was walking through the gate when the clock struck nine. The farmer's wife watched him approach then locked him out and he had to spend the night in the cow shed. "The good old days!" – I am not so sure, are you?'

◈ HARD WORK AND NOT MUCH MONEY ◈

'In 1895 Sam and Jane Furness came as tenants to Bubnell Farm, Baslow. One hundred years later the family is still there. Dairying has always been the mainstay of the farm business, milking by hand until the arrival of the milking machine in 1948. Hard work and not much money characterised farming in the 1930s. James remembers his father arguing fiercely with the milkman over the price per gallon. Their difference was one farthing! The coming of the Milk Marketing Board in 1933 was a life-line, providing a guaranteed market for all the milk produced.'

'I lived in the village of Longford as a child and my memories are mostly of my mother and how hard she worked. There was hand milking twice a day, and the milk had to be carried from the cowshed to the dairy and then tipped from buckets into a sieve higher than her head, before it ran down the cooler into the churn.

Laying hens were housed about a quarter of a mile away at the bottom of a steeply sloping field. They were tended by my mother about three times a day, once to let them out in the morning with corn and water carried down in large buckets, to feed and water them again in the afternoon, and then to shut them up in the evening. Yet despite all the work on the farm, our home was spotlessly clean.'

'My mother and father took over the tenancy of Swinholme Farm, Norbury, close by the river Dove in 1905. In the early years it was oil lamps, water from a pump in the yard, and hand milking. The milk was taken in four large churns by horse and cart to the cheese factory at Ellastone. By 1949, when my husband acquired a van, the milk went to the dairy at Uttoxeter. Sometimes a strike ensued, when agreement could not be reached regarding the milk prices. Then the farmers withheld their milk and cheese was made at home.

We employed a farm worker, who lived in a tied cottage, rent free. His wages were 38 shillings a week, with 2d a week deducted for the employee's share of the "Lloyd George" – the forerunner of the National Health Insurance stamp. He also had free milk, a row or two of potatoes and turnips from the field as required, and a share of the products of a pig killing.'

▣ GEORGIE THE TRAMP ▣

'My father had a small farm, along with ten or so others in the district. They were independent tenants of the Devonshire estates. Around the 1930s Georgie would turn up at the farm, suddenly out of the blue, and we would see him hanging over the wall near the house. He was used as an extra hand at sowing, harvest, threshing and winter turnip-pulling time. He would drift from farm to farm for very short spells. He was of medium height, stocky, aged around 30 years. He was often dirty, unshaven, with boils on his neck, string tied round his various garments and all his possessions were on his back. My father would provide a bucket of hot water, carbolic soap, shaving gear and old towels and despatch him to the stable for a tidy up. He was often given spare clothes. He was allowed into the farm kitchen for meals but sat at a slate sink with a clean tea-cloth under his food. He had a stupendous appetite!

Georgie listened to us a lot, stuttered when he had to reply but did not indulge in a lot of conversation. If pleased, he had a stupid but knowing grin on his face. I expect he was illiterate. We never knew where he slept, I suspect in the loft of a cow shed or stable or even a haystack. My father was very stern with him in that he never smoked there and threatened dire punishment. Georgie knew the "runs" to the workhouses of that time. He knew exactly which bus to catch to get him to Chesterfield, Worksop, Retford and Lincoln and the times for entry and departure from the workhouses. He worked farms *en route*.

My father never paid him until he had done the work required – two or three days involvement – as always he was gone next morning. He needed a fellow worker to keep him moving or, if unsupervised, he took a "rest".

As children we liked him, he was never sullen and never did us any harm. The family trusted him although I suspect my father watched him carefully. We were never allowed to tease him or be rude to him. I suppose the child in him found solace in us. I never heard him swear. He once told me his mother had turned him out.

I often wonder what happened to him – perhaps a hard winter became too much for him and his way of life. There were no hand-outs and Social Service claims for him. He was a character of the 1920s–1930s, never to be seen again.'

◙ FARM LIFE IN THE 1940S ◙

'Living in the village of Little Eaton as a child in the 1940s was an exciting time. One knew when the crop was ripe, it stood proud with splashes of red showing where the poppies grew and wild oats stood aloof, their heads high above the golden wheat. One also knew when it was time to harvest as a strip was cut around the field, with a scythe, wide enough to allow the binder to take the first cut.

It was a busy time in the village. First the wheat had to be cut; this was done by a binder which was pulled by horses, however tractors were now becoming more evident and took over the work. The binder cut the wheat, which fell onto canvas rollers; these carried it up to where it was tied into sheaves. Frequent breakages of the straps on the canvas sheets were experienced and the mechanism for tying the sheaves often broke, so frequent repairs, in the field, were necessary. The sheaves were then thrown out as the binder went on its way. This could be a time of great frustration if all did not go well, and it often did not.

The sheaves were then stood in stooks of eight to dry. This was done by hand and was back-breaking and dusty work. It was usual to pick up a sheaf in each arm and then place them on end; this job could be painful as the sheaves frequently contained thistles. When dry, the next stage was to carry the crop to the farm. This was a time of hard work and long days, ensuring the harvest was gathered in and neatly stacked to await the arrival of the threshing machine.

The arrival of the threshing machine was the start of another period of great activity. It was owned by one Harry Knifton, who lived in Milford, a nearby village. He used a steam traction engine to tow the threshing machine and baler around from village to village.'

'Threshing days meant hard and heavy work both in the stackyard at Inkersall Farm, Staveley and in the house where quantities of food and drink had to be provided for the men. When we children came down to breakfast there would be two or three unfamiliar, sooty-faced little men already sitting at the table. These were members of the Morgan family of Barlow who owned the huge threshing machine on which they rode to the farm on the first day. On subsequent days they walked from Barlow to Inkersall, a distance of about seven miles, before doing a day's work and then walked home again at night. The droning sound of the great steam engine which drove the threshing machine went on all day and sparks flew into the sky as more coal was shovelled on to keep the steam up. The men on the stack pitched the sheaves into the drum which banged and shook until the grain was beaten out of the ears of corn and collected into sacks. These sacks were carried on the men's shoulders up the wooden stairs into the corn loft above the barn.

My father would come into the house, with his eyes red and streaming from the chaff and dust which blew everywhere, to warn my mother that the men were ready, either for gallons of tea or a good hot dinner. This caused much hustle and bustle in the kitchen where all the cooking was done on open fires and side ovens without the luxury of electricity for fridges, freezers or cookers.

109

Tea in the harvest field at Bretby, and 'our first combine'.

Out in the stackyard, all was noise and activity at this culmination of the year's work, especially when the stack was almost down and boys with sticks and terriers waited for rats and mice which always came running out when there was nowhere left to hide. Shouts and barks mingled with the noise of the threshing machine.

Despite all the hard work, there was a feeling of great satisfaction as the cycle of the year turned once more and the golden grain was stored.'

▣ FARMING IN THE 1950S ▣

'My memories start with the ritual of milking as a dairy herd was kept. Although there were electric milking machines the men still sat on small three-legged wooden stools to hand strip the cows before the milking machines were brought into use and the ever present farm cats and their kittens would await their share of the warm rich milk. Horses were still used in the fields at Bretby, particularly at hay time, but the lofty stables were gradually put to other uses as the tractors took over. Men were still engaged hoeing and singling root crops by hand and potato picking was still a major event in October, usually coinciding with the school half term closure so that children could help in this mammoth event. I don't remember the jinny ring ever being used for winnowing but the three day visit of the threshing machine was always a very hectic time.

Gradually the pattern of farming changed. Horse-powered hay machines gave way to tractor-pulled implements and eventually a hay baler was acquired. The arrival of our first combine was a great day and was watched by many, particularly the sceptics who were convinced the machine could not do all that it was supposed to! I clearly remember writing a cheque for just over £2,000 – a huge sum – for our next combine. The advent of more powerful machinery began to do away with manual labour and there has been a consequent drop in the numbers employed. Today's men need to be technicians and skilled operators but it is good to think two of our original workers now cope with a considerably larger acreage while still having traditional skills such as hedge laying and ploughing very much part of their lives and that of the farm.'

'Seeing combines drive around the fields all over the country takes me back to the early days of threshing. For me, the farmer's wife, it began the day before. I cooked for ten hungry men. I cooked a large joint of brisket beef in my side oven. I then made three apple pies on large plates which were served with rice pudding. Coal to get in, rice to go in the oven. Next get potatoes and cabbage.

The engine man would arrive at 7 am to get the steam up. He would have a bacon sandwich. All the neighbouring farm labourers would arrive. We all helped one another. A jug of tea went out about ten o'clock with cups to bring back and wash up. I did have hot water on the sink. A bucket of potatoes (peeled the night before) and a bucket of cabbage to be cooked. Keep an eye on the rice pudding in the oven. Dinner at 12.30. Plates warmed, gravy to make. The table had an extension to seat ten. Some men washed their hands, others didn't. The amount of food put on plates was enormous. How they worked after, I don't know. Pudding eaten, then cups of tea, then back to work while I washed up, swept the floor of chaff. At 3.30 more cups of tea. They finished about 5 pm, all except the engine man, who came in for a sandwich.

I was taught this routine by my mother-in-law but my first time on my own, I remember, I had a six week old son to feed too. Was I tired. Those were the good old days when men and women worked hard. We were the first farm in our area to buy a trailer combine. Was I glad!'

VILLAGE TRADES AND CRAFTS

*V*illages were thriving centres of employment, services having
to be provided close to where people lived and worked in the days
before easy transportation. The village shop was at the heart of
the community, for goods and for gossip!

✤ THE SADDLER ✤

'In 1919 my father became an apprentice saddler after attending
the former grammar school in Tideswell. He served his five year
apprenticeship with Mr B. W. Palfreyman, a saddler of
Commercial Road, Tideswell. For the first month he worked
without pay to see if he was suitable for the job. Then for the first
year he was paid 5s a week and this went up to 9s weekly when
he was 20. At the end of his apprenticeship Mr Palfreyman wrote
him a reference and he went to work for Mr Frith, a saddler at 7
Market Street, Chapel-en-le-Frith, a business which had formerly
been owned by several generations of Bramwells. In 1925 he took
over the business and worked there alone until 1964.

In the early years he made sets of cart and trap harness, plough
pads, saddles and collars of various sizes, bridles, etc, using the
various knives and tools. In the summer months it was a night
and day job with farmers from the Chapel, Peak Forest, Hayfield
and New Mills areas bringing in their broken harness for repair,
as well as the canvas which had been damaged on their binders
when cutting corn.

My earliest memories are of a room full of large sides of leather
and its scent, and going in our Morris Eight car taking harness to
farms and delivering paraffin (used for lighting) which we also
sold.

After the war years the horses were gradually replaced by
tractors and motor cars, and leather by plastic, and the saddlery
trade deteriorated, so my father expanded into the hardware
trade. I recall people queueing on the day when the Pyrex ware,

enamel pans and buckets were to be delivered as they were in short supply.

On 5th November we sold fireworks which my brother and I had helped to wrap in newspaper in bundles of various prices for selling. These too were hard to come by. Some other articles he sold were cartridges and rabbit snares, nails, rope and wire netting. To measure a length of netting he would take the roll onto the footpath opposite the shop, roll it out and use each kerbstone as a measure, ie a stone was three feet in length. A frequent sight.

About 1958 the weekly cattle market in Chapel, which had been a busy and important factor in the town's life, closed, this affecting the business, so in 1964 the doors of the 200 year old shop closed.'

▨ THE BLACKSMITH ▨

'George Minion was the village blacksmith as was his father before him and the blacksmith's shop in the main street of Ticknall was always a hive of activity. The familiar sight in the smithy was of George wielding his big striking hammer on the anvil and his father, now getting on in years, operating the hand bellows which kept the fire glowing.

During the first half of the century, the blacksmith's services were in great demand. There were plenty of farm horses to be shod plus riding ponies, many of which were brought from the nearby villages of Repton and Melbourne for George Minion was a highly respected craftsman. Horses would stand tethered in Main Street waiting their turn whilst their keepers enjoyed a good gossip in the warmth of the blacksmith's shop. It was indeed known as the local gossip shop (for men!) and the village bobby was one of the most frequent visitors; it was not unknown also for the local bus to make an unscheduled stop outside and the driver to pop in for a warm.

In addition to shoeing horses, the blacksmith had plenty of farm implements to repair and local people would bring him their tools and even their buckets. The anvil also had another use – it served as the barber's chair and for the princely sum of 3d, the local men got a haircut!

114

Next door to the smithy was a farm and in one of its outbuildings lived a tramp known locally as "Desolate". Every morning he would go into the blacksmith's shop and make himself some toast on the fire – very black toast – and boil up water for his tea in an old Tarantella tomato tin. Not having too many opportunities for washing, he was not welcome to stay too long in working hours but spent those in the blacksmith's greenhouse where there was a small stove. To the children, he was not a figure to be feared except when he was drunk and then, so it is recalled, he was very nasty.

Despite being a very strong man, George Minion died suddenly in 1951, only 49 years of age. The previous day he had been digging a grave, yet another of his jobs in the village, and he was struck down by a virulent strain of flu. So ended the existence of a blacksmith's shop in Ticknall.'

◈ POST OFFICE AND SHOP ◈

'Midway through the 19th century a small shop which fronted onto Tibshelf High Street was bought as a drug store and by 1900 it also stocked grocery items and provisions. The village just had a telephone connection with towns and soon the shop housed the telephone exchange and the post office. The business had the telephone number 1 and this has been retained to this day, although five preceding digits have been added. Postal sorting and deliveries were arranged here, the mail bags being collected from the station and outgoing mail taken to the station each evening.

In 1900 the owner's son qualified as a chemist and took over management with his brother, and soon stabling was built for three horses. The business expanded with a salesman calling on farmers over a radius of several miles and horse-drawn vehicles made deliveries. At this time village families kept pigs in the sty in the garden and block salt was used to cure the pig meat and make bacon. This salt was bought in one ton lots. A contract was made to supply both collieries in the village with explosives and fuses and a special magazine was built well away from the shop. Now the chemist had a rising demand for patent medicines and

Regular deliveries from the corn merchant's van at Tibshelf.

bright new drawers held lots of herbal cures. Leeches to suck wounds clean were kept in a tank of water. Senna pods sold well, the shop purchased these in 28lb bags whilst bicarbonate of soda came in hundredweight sacks and was sold by the ounce either as a medicine or for baking.

By 1920 the shop was enlarged and later electricity was installed for lighting. This was provided by a paraffin-powered engine with a generator which ran for about ten hours each day. (It was also used to grind corn and charge the 20 accumulators storing power for night lighting.)

The store had frequent deliveries of animal feeds from Worksop by a steam and coal powered Foden lorry. Grocery customers preferred "tub butter" which came in hundredweight barrels, whilst flour and sugar were now purchased in tons. Flour was usually sold in stones (14lbs) and yeast (barm) cost one penny per ounce.

As telephone connections enlarged the 24 hour service made it necessary to move the exchange elsewhere and during the mid

1930s the shop was refitted. Farming was more profitable and the variety of groceries was greater, being stored in places called the "tea room", the "tin alley" and the "jam room". Deliveries were now made by van or lorry but this became very difficult during the Second World War.

The post war period saw the beginning of the National Health Service and again more space was needed so the post office was moved to other premises. There were now counters for the chemist, groceries, provisions, wines and spirits, and a department for the huge variety of animal feeds.'

'My home was a corner shop where my parents sold cakes, groceries, tobacco, beers, wines and spirits, sweets, cards, novelties, medicinal products, vegetables and fruit. The bananas came from the West Indies and arrived in crates that looked like slimline coffins. The bananas were packed in straw and occasionally there would be a very big spider lurking in the shadows.

Dad used to buy "loose" apricot wine. Customers would request a bottle of apricot wine, Dad would fetch a bottle, quickly rinse it out, fill the vessel with the fruity drink and then announce to the customer that he had sterilized the bottle first!'

'Mum made ice cream in a round wooden barrel with an inner lining. Ice would be put between the two, and the mixture in the centre of the barrel. There was a lid with a handle and she would stir and stir until the ice cream was set. It came out a lovely creamy yellow colour and a big cornet was one penny.'

❖ VILLAGE NEWS ❖

'"Just off to Ethel's" was a favourite call in Baslow, as many villagers made the daily stroll to collect their newspapers and magazines, but this was no ordinary visit, rather one of life's experiences to be amazed or amused by, depending on your views or experiences!

Ethel's shop was really a house. It fronted onto the main road through the village, accessible to everyone arriving on foot or by car (no aggravating parking restrictions in those carefree days), and to step inside her door was indeed a surprise. There was just sufficient room for three customers, more than three was a squeeze, and more than five had to queue outside. The complete "front room" was occupied by newspapers, from floor to ceiling, many of them vintage copies yellowed with age, some tied in bundles, some loose, but all cunningly arranged so that Ethel was able to have limited access to her "back room" which was her domestic living quarters. Here, in this tiny, cramped area, sat Miss Ethel Bufton, newsagent extraordinaire.

Miss Bufton was a tiny lady of indeterminate age, dressed always in black, so far as could be seen as only the upper part of her was visible above the counter of newspapers. She wore a shawl, only one in summer but as the cooler days arrived the shawls increased month by month. Some were quite grand, in mohair or delicately crocheted, others more antique, and on winter days she had to also wear mittens to help her fingers contend with the icy temperatures. There was, of course, no heating. Imagine the fire hazard, and in any case the fireplace had long since been obscured by newspapers. There was a piano in one corner – I saw its brass candelabra, now verdigris, but the piano too had become a good resting place for more piles of newspapers, as well as a snoozing place for her cats (there would be two or three there) all as antique as their surroundings.

Despite this seemingly haphazard world of business Miss Bufton was extremely capable with money matters. Her tin box of change, always well hidden, would be delved into for copper coins, the others kept separately in another tin box pushed carefully into a pile of newspapers well away from prying eyes. On quiet days, when villagers had been and gone with their dailies and weeklies, it was a good chance to have a chat with Ethel, about life, the world, her rheumatics, and best of all her early years with her dear mother.

The shop is empty now, and only memories remain, but Miss Bufton will be remembered not just for her eccentric way of living but for her generous bequest to St Anne's church in Baslow, and her many loyal years of "serving" as she handed over our newspapers.'

OTHER WAYS WE MADE A LIVING

From being in service to working for the Co-op, from pit ostler to railway signalman – these were just a few of the many other ways we earned a living.

◈ AT THE BIG HOUSE ◈

'When I was 14 years old I went to see Mr Carrington at Wye Bank, Rowsley. He was the estate agent for Haddon Estate. I was interviewed for a job on the estate chopping trees down, planting new trees etc. I started working with Hubert Evans and I had to report to Haddon Barn. Mr Twyford was the wood steward and I had to be at work for 7 am to 5 pm. We had one hour for dinner and finished Saturday at lunch time. That was 48 hours for 11s a week. I got 2s a week rise every year till I was 20 when I earned £1 per week. I then left to go to Millclove Mine, shift work in the lead smelting area. Seven days a week at 1s 3d per hour, just over £3 a week.

I enjoyed Haddon Estate very much. We planted a lot of the trees on the A6 in front of Haddon near the by-pass, or "road improvement" as it was called in those days. I remember going to the top of Church Lane, Rowsley to see Mr Twyford; his son Fred was leaving Haddon and he asked me if I would like to work in the gardens. Mr Stanhope from Bridge Street, Bakewell was in charge. We used to mow lawns, keep borders tidy etc.

When I was about 17 years old I moved into Haddon Hall to work with the indoor staff. My duties included feeding the dogs and carrying coal and logs to bunkers in all the rooms. These wicker baskets were lined with metal. I also used to soften the water which pumped from the river Derwent to a large tank above Haddon. Then the water was in a large boiler at the top of the courtyard. I would put about ten drops of liquid in the water to soften it. When the family were in residence I used to feed the dogs around 1 pm, when the family had lunch. I would take the

Oct 15·1934

This is to certify that I have known John Shimwell for the past ten years. He passed thro our Schools satisfactorily & I believe him to be a fair scholar. For the last six years he has been in the Service of his Grace the Duke of Rutland at Haddon Hall & I have reason to know has given entire satisfaction. His habits are regular. I believe him to be hard working, truthful, honest, & sober.

A reference written for John Shimwell in 1934 after he had been in the service of the Duke of Rutland.

dogs, three golden retrievers and a bulldog, and the kitchen staff would give me a stock to mix with the dog biscuits. We would have our dinner in the servants' quarters, which is now a restaurant; 29 would sit down. The butler and the lady's maid sat at the top and bottom of the table and their names were Mr and Mrs Keenan, who had apartments at the bottom courtyard.

One day I was cleaning the chapel and using a brush to clean the walls, when some of the plaster fell off and underneath were parts of paintings. I called Mr Stanhope and they found beautiful paintings underneath – now everyone can see them.

We also used to go beating for the family for the shooting season. The Duke and Duchess also had homes at Belvoir, London and Scotland. When they were at Haddon I often saw nobility, Dame Laura Knight and the Prince of Wales, before he became the Duke of Windsor. These are very happy memories.'

❖ The Silversmith ❖

'No 56 Howard Street was a shabby, dull, brick building which housed my family's silversmithing business, and had stood in that role since just before 1900. It was surrounded by other smog-encrusted works of equal vintage. From the outside its only redeeming feature was the shop window displaying a variety of silverware, always attractive to the passerby, more especially on gloomy winter days when the well-lit window was the only bright attraction on the dusty city street.

Inside the shop, divided into separate rooms, was brightly lit, lined with glass cupboards, and these were packed with more silverware, tea-services, cake trays, cutlery, rose bowls and all manner of luxury items of the day. Across a narrow passage, gloomy and ill-lit, was the inner sanctum, known as "the office". Here my grandfather, a rotund figure, rosy-cheeked, with a fringe of white hair, his spectacles tied with string and pushed high on his forehead when not in use, would spend most of his working day, and late into the night too. He was a skilled silversmith and engraver, and would pore over items of silver, some antique, some modern, often seeking an even closer look with his jeweller's monocle manoeuvred to one eye. He would design pieces for engraving and pierced work (looking like filigree patterns) and his knowledge of hall-marks, always incised on every item of silver, was immense.

Being absorbed in his own world, he never made much in the way of greeting as I wandered in, but I knew I had to do my greeting to him! I loved him dearly but dreaded to kiss him on account of his splendid but wickedly sharp waxed moustache. This he would, from time to time, delicately twirl at either end ensuring it was always pin-sharp. Many times I rushed to his side, gave the obligatory peck to his cheek, then hastily withdrew before he had time to respond, leaving my cheek with a sharp pricking sensation which I tried to rub quickly before he noticed!

A flight of rickety wooden steps outside led to the buffing shop. Here three "buffer girls", all middle-aged women, worked all day on pieces of silverware. Every aspect of this work was done by hand, their fingers meticulously smoothing jeweller's rouge into every part of the item. Indeed the smoothness of their fingertips was vital to the work as each piece of silverware was buffed until smooth as silk. The workplace was old-fashioned, decades of dust everywhere, no heating, yet they shared a companionship over the years that it would be hard to find nowadays. I was required not to touch on any account, so chatted and watched, intrigued by this atmosphere so far removed from home or school.'

❖ A SHOP ON THE SPOT ❖

'As a child in the late 1930s I spent a lot of my time at my grandparents' shop on the Spot in Derby. It was a fascinating place, built over many small cellars of previous buildings. In 1900 it had belonged to "Burton Wine & Spirits" and when the sun shone through the windows you could see where the white enamel letters had been.

It was definitely a shop for the less affluent, selling all kinds of things, and we had a Pot Club. Clubholders collected money weekly, sixpence or a shilling, from customers and received a ticket in exchange ranging from five shillings to £1, with the tenth weekly collection given to the clubholders as commission. Lots of girls collected their bottom drawer in this way. Occasionally even now people say that their steps or colander or whatever was from Freeman's Pot Club and is still going strong.

Goods were usually delivered by LMS drays with beautiful shire horses. We always had a supply of carrots or apples to give them, sometimes pushed through the side of a muzzle – some of them would bite. The draymen had a love/hate relationship with their horses. Sometimes the horses would stop at the shop door for a titbit even if they had no delivery and the draymen started shouting – they had a wide-ranging vocabulary.

During the war goods were in very short supply. I would travel with my mother down the Lye or to the Potteries buying whatever we could. The following day (it must have been jungle telegraph) queues would form outside the shop to buy a saucepan or kettle, only one article per person. We sold them from skips at the back of the shop, no time to unpack them, and I had to run up and down to the cash till for change.

They don't have this kind of old-fashioned shop any more but I remember it with great affection. I also remember it was very hard work!'

Looking busy in the Control Room of the Midland Railway.

▣ ON THE RAILWAY ▣

'Derby had two railway apprentice training schools. The first, the Locomotive Works Apprentice Training School, started training first year craft trainees in 1947 and was located in the heart of the Derby Locomotive Works. Many years earlier the Training School building was described by locomen as the "Piano Shop" because of the many blacksmith's hammers tapping on the anvils.

1956 saw the official opening of the Litchurch Lane Works Training School. It stood on the periphery of the sprawling works and was accommodated in a substantial two-storey building that in its earlier days saw the manufacture and repair of signalling equipment.

The main purpose of the training schools was to ensure an adequate number of suitable apprentices who would carry on the highly skilled trades involved in railway engineering. Those trainees who were Loco School trained were biased towards metal engineering skills. Trainees who entered the Litchurch Lane Training School had a wide choice of vehicle building skills, wood, paint and trimming skills in addition to the metal skills. There were eight trades in the Loco School and 13 in the Litchurch Lane School.

Eventually, eleven more training schools were spawned from the two Derby ones. First Aid training was conducted in all of them and many were the keenly contested competitions. Sadly the schools no longer function. The last one closed in 1986 approximately.'

'My father was special. In the 1920s when many were unemployed, he had a regular, responsible job as railway signalman. Trains ran on time and safely. Not much more than £2 per week was his income, including night shifts, but there was a bonus. Free passes and quarter fares gave us access to distant parts of the country on express steam trains going at 60 miles per hour, or there were stopping trains linking nearer towns.

The signal boxes were draughty, cold places, warmth coming from a well-stoked coal fire with a small oven. A load of fuel would be supplemented with huge lumps of best Yorkshire or Welsh coal dropped from an engine stopped at a nearby signal. Opening windows were on three sides of the box. The levers had slots to slide in, and in the lower level the wires travelled through gaps to the signals. There was no loft or insulation and double glazing hadn't become part of our language.

Just before the war, Dad moved up a grade to a signalbox with huge wooden crossing gates controlled by a large wheel, gaining five shillings per week rise, plus more overtime. The pay was calculated on lever movements rather than responsibility. After the retreat from Dunkirk when there was a serious threat of invasion by the Germans, Dad started putting the very long poker into the fire at night, keeping the end red hot as his only weapon to defend the crossing.

Visits to New Mills to my mother's aunt entailed two, sometimes three stopping trains each way, clicking along at a leisurely pace, with the porter at each station taking charge of the tickets, the gas lamps glowing on the return journey.'

⬧ OIL IN THE COALFIELDS ⬧

'In the early years of this century geological conditions and oil seepages into collieries showed that there might be oil in the area of the North Derbyshire Coalfields. After a countrywide survey eleven trial bore holes were drilled in the British Isles. Seven of these were in Derbyshire. Only one well proved to have oil in a commercial quantity and that was between Tibshelf and Hardstoft. It was known as Tibshelf/Hardstoft No 1 Well though within the Tibshelf village boundary.

Oil was struck at a depth of 3,077 feet on the night of 27th May 1919, and it flowed during the following June. The oil was of excellent quality from this first mainland well in Britain, it resembled Pennsylvanian Crude and was very suitable for cylinder lubrication. For almost eight years around 250 gallons were extracted each day and during the first four years the oil flowed from this well by its natural pressure. When this flow reduced more was extracted by pumping. In 1938 a specialist oil company was engaged and production increased for several years until 1945 when the oil almost dried up.

The plant, which produced roughly 3,500 tons (28,000 US barrels) of crude oil, was demolished in 1952, and the well was capped.

It still seeps a little oil.'

⬧ STOCKINGERS, CHEVENING AND COAL ⬧

'I heard of George Stephenson's connection with Crich when I was a child. He, of *Rocket* fame, helped found the Clay Cross Company. He lodged in Crich, at the Wheatsheaf Inn, while superintending the construction of the mineral railway from the Cliff Quarry, where the Tramway Museum now is, to the Clay Cross lime kilns at Ambergate.

The line ran along the west side of the village, under the escarpment of the Tors. This was a sandstone area which sloped gradually towards the Derwent valley at Whatstandwell, but presented the cliff face of the escarpment towards the village of Crich.

The little steam engine *Dowey* pulled twelve small wagons,

126

loaded with limestone to the lip of the valley where there was a steep drop to the lime kilns. Here the wagons were unhitched and sent, six at a time, on an endless rope down to the kilns, at the same time pulling up six empty wagons, to return them all to the quarry. Not all the wagons came up empty, some were full of coal which was sold to villagers at the quarry entrance.

People bought one or two hundredweights at a time. It was put into small trucks, about three feet by two feet, made of very thick wood. Each truck had two small iron wheels and a long iron handle with a loop at the end.

The coal was usually fetched by boys. This was not a great hardship as it was downhill all the way from the quarry to home. The only danger was if the truck ran away with a boy on a steep hill, but if he let go of the handle the truck tipped forward and the bottom edge scraped the ground, acting as a brake.

From the late 18th century there were many stocking-frame workers in Crich. In the centre of the village there are three-storey stone houses. The top storey has a long window made up of many little panes, this is the room where the stockingers worked. There used to be a number of cottages with these long

Lea Mills in about 1910.

windows; there were several on Workhouse Row, which had nothing to do with the Poor Law, it was simply the row of cottages where the stockingers worked.

They used to fetch the yarn from the supplier, often walking as far as Ilkeston to collect it and the money for the stockings they had taken in. I heard elderly men say when they were paid they had a day or two drinking then had to work all hours to knit up the yarn and earn more money.

The workers often had a glass ball, about four inches in diameter, full of water, hanging in the window. This was to focus the light of the sun or a candle on the work when some intricate work, like picking up a dropped stitch, was in process.

In a cottage at the Town End lived, in 1914, an old man who had been a stockinger. Someone took him and his frame to London and set him up to work in a shop window, for a week. He was amazed that London folk came to watch him doing what to him was normal work.

A Fritchley family named Leafe built a large, substantial stone workroom in the garden of their cottage, with a long window on the south side. There the brothers worked for years until Marsden Smedley opened the Lea Mills hosiery factory, and they went to work there.

In the 1930s King George VI visited Lea Mills. He was presented with two little knitted swimsuits for the two princesses. He promptly ordered swimming trunks for all the boys in the summer camps he organised, where public school boys met boys from working class homes. This order caused great excitement in the area. Much overtime work was needed to fulfil the order in time, and retired workers like Mr Leafe were called back to help.

In the early years of this century men's woollen socks had a line of silk embroidery up the side from the ankle. This was called chevening and the work was hand-done by women working in their homes.

My paternal grandmother, her daughter and my cousin all did chevening. They lived in Riddings, and fetched the socks in bundles of a gross pairs, from stocking factories at Leabrooks and Alfreton.

Grandma's parlour was at the back of her cottage, overlooking the garden. The sofa was positioned across the corner near the fireplace, so that sitting on it the workers had a good light over their shoulders onto the work. The big bag of socks was hidden behind the sofa.

The embroidery silk, and it was silk not mercerised cotton, was supplied by the factory. The cheveners used a different needle for each colour, and parked their needles on the wide decorative cloth which hung round the mantelpiece.

The sock was pulled over the left hand, a line was scratched with the needle and then quickly a satin stitch line was worked from the ankle for about six inches. The top was finished with a sprat's head.'

☼ THE PIT OSTLER ☼

'As children my brother and I lived in the pit houses which were situated between the pit-heads, one at the top and two at the bottom of the row. There were 32 houses in the row. My father was employed at the pit as the ostler. He worked twelve-hour shifts and finished his week's work at one o'clock on Saturday.

His duties included delivering the allowance coal by horse and cart to the miners who lived in the row, shovelling it onto the cart and then unloading it into the miners' coal houses; fetching loads of clay from down a country lane, which would be used in the pits by the shot-firers; in the winter when it snowed, working all night with the horse and wooden snow plough to keep the road open so the miners could get to work; caring for the ponies when they came out of the pit for the fortnight's holiday. One of the highlights of his life was taking a pit pony to the Horse of the Year Show and meeting the Queen.'

☼ THE INDUSTRIAL NURSING SERVICE ☼

'In 1946 I was employed as an Industrial Nurse by the engineering and mining Butterley Company of Ripley. After

Arthur Clapton, pit ostler, and one of his ponies meet the Queen at the Horse of the Year Show.

being introduced to the Company Doctor and the Head Nursing Officer I learned of the many collieries and engineering plants owned by the Butterley Company and of some of their past achievements, notably the roof of St Pancras station and much of the iron works of Dover docks. I was then taken round some of the collieries and iron foundries. This was my first glimpse of the face of heavy industry. I was appalled and somewhat intimidated by the continual deafening noise, the all prevailing dust and the conditions of discomfort, all of which the men appeared to accept as a matter of course.

Next day I was installed in a very basic first aid room on one of the larger pit tops; after the sterile conditions of my training hospital, the open fire and the impossibility of keeping the coal dust from seeping in caused me some anxiety. However, I soon learned to accept this along with the somewhat sceptical attitude of many miners who considered a woman on the pit a harbinger of bad luck – in the appallingly dangerous conditions of pre-nationalisation mining, the miners needed any luck available to survive.

As I became more accustomed to the demands of industrial nursing my admiration for the mining community grew. Their quick humour and solidarity in supporting each other under conditions of often intolerable cold, wet and danger amazed me, as did their stoical acceptance of the pain of numerous injuries and disabilities inherent in this occupation.

Due to family commitments I had a 20 year break, then, with a grown up family, returned to the Colliery Nursing Service with a feeling of coming home. By this time the coal industry had been nationalised for 18 years and the facility of a well equipped and fully staffed surgery at the colliery site had become an accepted and valued fact. As Colliery Nursing Sister I was treated with much kindness and unfailing courtesy and I felt very much part of the community. I became involved in training for the St John Ambulance personnel. No colliery would have been able to function without the presence of a trained St John Ambulance man on every coal face.

Most of the social life of the community centred around the Miners' Welfare Club. The colliery villages always seemed to me like a large extended family and while I worked at the colliery I felt honoured to be included in their many activities.'

❧ TEACHER TRAINING DURING THE WAR ❧

'I was fortunate to be accepted for teacher training at the Diocesan Training College in 1944. Being wartime the age of admission had been lowered to 17. The ATS had commandeered the college buildings on Uttoxeter Road, Derby and our first year as students was spent at Elvaston Castle.

Night life was non-existent; the most daring thing we did was to cycle to nearby Borrowash and return with a music satchel bulging with chips (strictly forbidden food!).

Life was hard and extremely primitive in comparison with present day standards. I still shiver when I recall those early morning washes in Stone Bathroom (aptly called) after

Opposite: *The first aid room at New Langley Colliery in 1944,* and Above: *A doctor's treatment room.*

descending around 60 stone steps – not be be recommended on a freezing January morning!

Six of us shared a bedroom at the top of the castle. I was grateful for the company of my fellow students, as doors and windows creaked and owls hooted eerily.

There were numerous rules and regulations in those far off days and woe betide anyone who transgressed. Boy friends were only allowed to visit if they had been introduced (and approved) by the Principal, Miss H. K. Hawkins.

The food was very monotonous. Stuffed marrow, kippers and watery porridge figured large on the menu. Supper never varied – bread and dripping and cocoa. Parcels from home were much appreciated, especially if they contained sweet coupons.

Being a church college we were expected to attend daily

Students put on A Midsummer Night's Dream in 1945 at Elvaston Castle.

services in the beautiful Elvaston church, situated in the grounds of the castle.

A highlight of the year was a production of *A Midsummer Night's Dream*, in the idyllic setting of the lake and surrounded by the beautiful mature trees. Alas! on the appointed day there was a violent thunderstorm and the dream turned into a nightmare! This was our organized drama production but we had great fun from the sketches and songs we composed for "Party Nights". These were all female occasions!'

▣ MEMORIES OF MEDICINE ▣

'My father Dr F. W. Schofield came to Derby in 1930 to join Dr Southern's practice in Friargate. The practice employed a dispenser and a chauffeur. Dr Southern refused to drive the early motor cars known as "bone-shakers" in case the constant shudder of the steering wheel upset his delicate surgeon's touch. When my father took on the practice he employed the chauffeur as a gardener and his wife as a nursemaid for his children. My mother also had a living-in cook.

Bad debts were a common problem. "How kind of Mrs So and So to give us a pot of jam," enthused my mother.

"Yes dear," replied my father. "But I wish she'd pay her bill instead!"

The war years similarly were very hard for my father. His brother and partner Dr Barlow Schofield was called up so he struggled on by himself and was constantly overworked.

Income in the Derby practice was dependent on private patients. Changes in 1948 due to the coming of the National Health Service resulted in the doctor receiving payment related to the number of registered patients in the practice. My father moved back into Derby from Duffield to cut down on travelling time and attend more patients. Neither doctor had a son or daughter who wished to enter medicine and eventually the practice was divided between other doctors in the city. However, older visitors to Pickfords House Museum in Derby will recognise the original site of Dr Southern's surgery and consulting rooms.'

'After qualifying as a doctor in 1933 my fiancée and I decided on general practice in the country. In those days consultants all lived close to the hospitals where they worked. I viewed three practices before I came to see Baslow. I liked Dr Edleston, Chatsworth House was in the practice and the countryside was attractive. The practice was very run down due to the protracted illness of Dr Edleston the previous winter so the purchase price of two years' gross takings was modest.

The surgery was a wing built on to the doctor's house in 1908. It consisted of three rooms, a consulting room, a waiting room and in between a small dispensary. The latter supplied all the patients. The surgery hours seemed reasonable, 8.30–9 am and 5.30–6 pm but the waiting room outer door was only unbolted between these times. There was no appointment system so at 9 am and 6 pm there was a room full of patients, requiring at least two hours to attend to their needs. In early years there was no ancillary help and not even a telephone in the consulting room. Most requests for visits arrived on scraps of paper sometimes barely legible. A visit to Chatsworth could take half a morning by the time you had seen the patient, interviewed the housekeeper and spoken to a member of the family.

There was no ambulance service except for a ramshackle vehicle in Eyam, only available to subscribers of five shillings per person per annum. All confinements were at home, time consuming and a source of worry. Complicated cases were referred to the Jessop Hospital in Sheffield. The Panel Committee paid a small quarterly sum according to the number of registered panel patients which was relatively small in a country area. In early years I relied on private practice for most of my income. The wage earner was covered by the Panel but not his wife and dependants. In 1935 a consultation and an eight ounce bottle of medicine cost half a crown. Bad debts were rife and I employed a debt collector who called on the debtors once a week for one shilling. Eventually he absconded with some of the takings. Every winter we expected to lose four or five fathers of families with pneumonia.

During the war I was on call every night and every weekend. As time went on it was clear to me that general practice was deteriorating. In 1942 Sir William Beveridge published his recommendations and plans for a National Health Service which would protect everyone from "the womb to the tomb". At last I could discern light at the end of the tunnel. In the postwar Labour Government Aneurin Bevan succeeded in putting the service into action but it took a number of years to rescue general practice from the "slough of despond".'

▨ WORKING FOR THE CO-OP ▨
'Between the years of 1948 and 1953 I worked at the Hathersage Branch (Branch 21) of the Sheffield and Ecclesall Co-operative Society in the Hope Valley.

I started work as an assistant in the busy grocery shop, when rationing was still on for provisions – butter 2oz, sugar 4oz, margarine 4oz, lard 2oz, cheese 3oz, bacon 5oz per person per week. Tea and soap were still on coupons. The butter came in large barrels and the sugar in sacks. We spent hours weighing up these items; weighing the sugar was a sticky job, crunching under your feet and horrible if it got into your shoes. We generally did the weighing up on Monday. Bacon had to be boned (not very pleasant in hot weather especially if the flies had got to it and laid their eggs). I'm afraid hygiene wasn't too strict in those days. Any bread left over a weekend or bank holiday was soaked in a bowl of cold water and put in the hot oven to freshen it up.

After I had been at work for about 18 months I was sent out on my bike to collect in the weekly orders. You went to the customer's house, collected their order (hopefully already written out in a little book) and they paid for the previous week's order. Also some customers joined the Trading Club, usually for buying clothes, shoes etc: for £5 worth of stamps you paid five shillings per week for 20 weeks.

I used to travel to Castleton Monday mornings to collect the order for the top half of Hope village. Monday afternoon and Tuesday morning I collected the bottom half of the village and along the Edale Road. Tuesday afternoon I collected the village of Bamford, Wednesday morning I collected Hope Road and Thornhill then over the lonely lane to Yorkshire Bridge (by the Ladybower dam). Later in the afternoon I returned to the shop with some of the order books (the ones from previous calls had been collected from my home by the van). On my return to the shop I now had to price up the order books and help to put up the orders and parcel up the groceries in brown paper tied with string. This was a work of art. Thursday morning I was back again on the road, cycling to Grindleford and Padley.

When I think back, I was responsible for money amounting to £300 to £400, which was a lot of money in those days, all carried around in a tin case (with a hole in the top corner, obviously dropped by a previous colleague), a St Bruno tobacco tin for loose change and a tatty leather wallet for the notes. There were some very lonely roads to travel on for a girl of 16 years and some very strange customers to deal with. I wouldn't do it now.

Thursday afternoon I returned to the shop. It was a busy afternoon as the lorry arrived with the new stock, also we had to get together Friday's delivery of groceries to Bamford, Yorkshire Bridge and outlying farms.

Friday saw me back on the road again, this time on the van. Apart from Bamford and Yorkshire Bridge we had to visit farms around the Ladybower and Derwent dams, then up towards the Snake Pass over the moors to Lockerbrook Farm. Here we had a lovely welcome, a hot cup of tea waiting for us, the groceries unpacked and paid for. The lovely big tea cakes we'd just delivered were spread with home-churned butter and to sit by a lovely open fire for a warm before you set off again was lovely.

In winter we would often get the van stuck in the snow and have to start and dig out, especially on the hill tops, often having to leave the van and carry the goods on our backs in the very deep snow. If we got stuck in the villages we went and fetched the dustbins from nearby houses and emptied the ashes under the wheels.

It was often nine o'clock on a Friday night when I returned home from work, all for 37s 6d a week. I really wouldn't have missed it – more exciting than sitting pushing groceries along a conveyor belt.'

⬧ HARD TIMES ⬧

'As a child I remember most Willington men worked at the Bass brewery. Every day they walked to work, spent all day hard at work, then walked home again, ten miles I would think. The family next door had 16 children, all well dressed on one brewery worker's wage.

My husband's family were tenants (in a nearby village) of the local squire. He would never allow a car on his land, only horse power. He was very strict and my father-in-law having shot a rabbit and been found out, had to apologise, almost on bended knee, in fear of being put out of his cottage.'

'At Brimington, near Chesterfield, my father was a miner with four children. In 1926 the General Strike broke out, first the miners, then railways and industries, but the latter went back after a short time and the miners continued for many weeks. He was a militant and was therefore blacklisted. He did not get a job even when others started. There was no strike pay so he eventually got unemployment money – about 25 shillings a week.

When the strike was on the children were sent to the Salvation Army for breakfast (bread, dripping and tea). The Wesleyan chapel at Staveley gave teas of bread and jam. Father riddled coal from a former colliery tip and got slack – small pieces of coal and dust. He grew as many vegetables as possible. He soled the family's shoes. Food consisted of a cheap joint on Sunday that stretched to shepherd's pies in the week. One dinner was a casserole of potatoes and onions. Supper was cocoa made with water. Bread was home-baked and jam was made from brambles. Clothes were patched and handed down, finally ending in rag rugs. Christmas luxury was a pork joint, definitely no alcohol or tobacco. There was real poverty with little government aid, but most people were practical and ingenious.'

'Before the war the men's occupations at Youlgreave were farming, mining or quarrying. For the quarry workers, life was very hard in the winter months. Often they could not work because of ice, frost or snow. Then there was no money coming in to feed the family, and many a farmer turned a blind eye to those taking turnips and potatoes from their fields. One mother of a large family was well known for her ability to tickle trout. People were aware of her mission when she walked down the dale with a certain neighbour who was her lookout!'

WAR & PEACE

MEMORIES OF
THE GREAT WAR 1914–1918

The war was fought far away from Derbyshire, but one lady remembers the fear brought by the Zeppelin raids, the wounded soldiers on the streets and the dreadful flu epidemic which followed the war.

'I was born on the tenth day of the tenth month, 1913. I can picture sitting in front of a glowing fire watching Mother shaking a glass bottle round and round attempting to make a little butter from the cream skimmed off the milk. A brown pottery mug was also filled for my supper; the big treat being to skim off the cream with a thin arrowroot biscuit before drinking it.

Although very young, "little pigs have big ears" and I picked up bits of grown-up conversation. The word on everyone's lips was Zeps! My father worked in the control room on No 1 platform at Derby station, nerve centre of the Midland Railway as it was known then. He was on night duty when the Zeppelins came over Derby to bomb Chaddesden sidings.

Although I didn't quite realise what it was all about at the time, I remember being bundled into a green eiderdown and taken next door where everyone was sitting around, the only illumination being one lighted candle. I recall Father saying in later years that if only he'd had his air rifle with him, he'd have taken a pot shot at the "So and So".

There was much talk of wounded soldiers and Red Cross nurses and I have a faded snapshot of myself dressed as a Red Cross nurse and carrying a small metal crocodile-grained case, containing a rag doll in the blue hospital uniform, a quantity of bandages and pink lint – which must have kept me occupied for hours. Both my uniform and the soldier were made by my mother, as were my hand-knitted socks. Indeed, she made all our clothes.

Little Nancy dressed as a Red Cross nurse during the First World War.

Another very vivid picture that remains with me concerns the deadly flu epidemic that followed in the aftermath of war. We lived in Coronation Villas (now a row of shops) on the London Road, Alvaston. Shardlow is two to three miles away; here there

Volunteer Force

To

○ 3,11583 Pte. William Morris Upton.

I am commanded by The King to express to you
His Majesty's thanks for the services which you have
rendered to the Nation during the great War as an
enrolled Volunteer in the

7th V. Bn. Notts & Derby Regt.

Winston S. Churchill

Secretary of State for War.

Certificate of Service

Enrolled *19. 2. 18* .   Discharged *19. 10. 19.*

Entered into an Agreement under the Volunteer Act, 1916, on *19. 2. 18*
to continue serving in the Force for the duration of the War, and to perform the
prescribed programme of training.

Entered into an Agreement under the Volunteer Act, 1916, on ———
to perform temporary Service.

Served as a full=time soldier with a Volunteer Special Service Company
from ——— 1918, to ——— 1918.

Official thanks from the King for volunteer soldier, William Upton of the Notts & Derby Regiment.

was a workhouse (since become a hospital). Daily we would witness a few ragged, struggling souls trying to make their way there.

One such victim was seen by my mother holding onto the railings in front of our house. I was told in no uncertain manner not to go out of the house. She then took an old wooden chair from the kitchen and gave him a mug of tea. It transpired that he was an old soldier. I was looking out of the window and shall never forget the peculiar colour of his face, the look that said "Thank you", but the over-riding air of despair and hopelessness. The chair was subsequently scrubbed with disinfectant and left outside.

I believe this awful epidemic accounted for as much loss of life, if not more, than the First World War itself.'

THE SECOND WORLD WAR 1939–1945

Some 20 years later war came again, this time affecting every part of our lives. Rationing, the blackout, incendiary and high explosive bombs – through it all life went on.

⬛ BOMBS ON DERBY ⬛

'When the war started everyone expected raids immediately, but in fact these did not happen. However, I remember a one-off raid in the first year of the "phoney" war, when unequipped with any kind of shelter, our small family huddled downstairs behind the settee in case of flying glass, while with a deafening noise bombs were dropped on a neighbouring avenue near the City Hospital, flattening one house and killing its occupants.

Not very long after this, I was summoned, when in my early teens, into the Derbyshire Royal Infirmary for a minor operation. Unfortunately it was at this time that a raid was carried out on the Midland Railway station. In a post-operative haze, my bed with many others was trundled down to the cellars, with the great lagged pipes overhead. I believe operations were conducted down there while the raid continued.

I remember the food I had while in hospital – no menus in those days! A lot of bread and butter for breakfast and tea with an egg if one was brought in by a visitor; chicken and jelly for lunch immediately after the operation, but mince and rice pudding thereafter. I've never been able to stand minced meat since then!'

'I was 14 when war broke out. I started on the railway as a shorthand typist at Derby Midland station when I was nearly 15, having passed an entrance examination, and my wage to begin with was 7s 6d per week. I remember us all having to wear gas masks every Monday morning while we typed and then we were ushered down to the cellars in a very orderly manner for air raid drill.

Every Wednesday lunch time we enjoyed Workers' Playtime concerts at the Railway Institute – there was a pianist, singer and comedian, and this was their wartime effort to go around giving these concerts as morale boosters.

My father was an air raid warden so when the sirens went, almost every night, he donned his tin hat and government issue blue boiler suit and went out complete with stirrup pump ready to put out any incendiary bombs which Jerry had a habit of dropping. It was during these air raids that my mother, two sisters and myself made a quick descent into an air raid shelter which was the brainchild of a railway engineer who lived two doors away, so the occupants of four houses shared this "dug out". We sat huddled together on benches in masses of warm clothing worn over our night attire and supped numerous hot drinks from flasks prepared before we went to bed. A great spirit of camaraderie prevailed in that shelter although every time the Jerry planes came over we held our breath and were always glad to hear the "all clear" siren.'

'I came to Derby from Hull to take up a new post in the infants' school at Normanton, on 1st September 1939. I arrived in the blackout and was to stay in the YWCA hostel in Green Lane. I

146

had no idea where it was and was standing with my luggage feeling helpless when a new recruit in battledress (the train had been full of them) offered to walk me there and carry my bag. I accepted without a qualm, and when we had done the long walk to Green Lane my friendly escort offered me a date for the next evening. He was stationed in Curzon Street barracks. Rather ungratefully I did not agree to meet him – after all I couldn't see his face in the blackout, but I hope he survived the war.

The next day was Saturday so I looked round Derby which seemed small and homely after the city of Hull. The new Council House was being built and opposite was that lovely old Mayor's Parlour long since vanished. I remember Cockpit Hill with cobbles and market stalls and the narrow entrance into Eagle Street and then Devonshire Street where I later taught in the old St Peter's church school. I also worked in the big old school in Traffic Street which took all the children from the slums of Siddals Road, Borroughs Walk, Castle Place etc. The families were desperately poor and shockingly housed.

I remember the barrage balloons, one of which was anchored on waste ground at the top of Babington Lane. I think that was the one that broke loose and caused considerable havoc. I also recall the very unpleasant suffocating fumes from the smoke-screen burners between the town and Rolls-Royce. Very effective but extremely unpleasant if in the street outside your front door.'

'During the war Normanton Park had a barrage balloon, which was replaced by an anti-aircraft gun which made a horrendous noise when it went off. Our house in Chatsworth Street was damaged by the shrapnel from the gun, not from enemy action.

Warwick Avenue and Carlton Road had smoke-screen canisters which were lit on moonlit nights (in an attempt to hide Rolls-Royce, the railway and sidings and other industrial firms). Often these caught fire and were then more of a danger than useful. The smell was vile. A large static water tank was built in Clarence Road school grounds.'

147

Peace returns to Derby – St Mary's Gate in 1948.

A Good Use for Chatsworth

'In preparation for war, the tenth Duke and Duchess of Devonshire were told that their spacious home, like many others, must be put to good use. Negotiations were made for a girls' boarding school, Penrhos College from Colwyn Bay, to take over Chatsworth House, and they stayed until 1946. Meanwhile Penrhos College was commissioned to be used as a safe haven for the Ministry of Food.

The Duke and Duchess and family moved to Churchdale Hall at Ashford in the Water. It is hard to imagine all the packing of treasures, pictures and tapestries, as well as the arrival of beds and equipment for about 300 girls, including 26 pianos, all in eleven days.

Although in the relative safety of Derbyshire, Chatsworth House did receive some war damage. During 1942 the north side was hit by German bombers. It was revealed much later that they were out to bomb the DP factory in Bakewell which made batteries for submarines, and had followed the route of the Derwent river instead of the Wye. One of those planes flew low over my home, and I can still see that pilot's face, and the markings on the plane – I was eight years old.'

The Long Dark Night

'The year was 1940, in the dark days before Christmas. I arrived home from school, Dad was preparing dinner, for our mum was now working in Nottingham to help the war effort. My first job, before it got too dark, was to collect doctor's prescriptions for my elderly uncle and aunt from the chemist in Sandiacre about half a mile away. Returning, it was now dark and there seemed to be no one about, no street lights, no shop lights, only the occasional darkened bus and even cycle lamps could only show a tiny half light.

Mission accomplished and on my way home, then, shrilling through the darkness came the sound of the Carr Fastener factory air raid siren, ooh, ooh, ooh, it went. Followed by the one from Sandiacre and then Stanton Ironworks buzzer, a very deep noise, it seemed to chase me home. The searchlights were now sweeping across the skies.

149

Back home, still no mother. We could now hear the drone of the enemy aircraft and Dad was worried as he had to leave for work, a night shift, by 9 pm. He banked up the fire and replaced the fireguard, always a must. Perhaps my aunt could come and stay with me and my younger sister until Mum came home? However, she could not help as relatives had just arrived by train from Sheffield. Having been bombed out, they were cold and bedraggled, needing hot food and warm dry beds, all of which had to be organised.

The all clear went, by now it was getting foggy and frosty. Dad went to work, we were alone. However, about midnight, Mum was banging on the door. When I let her in, what a sight she looked, frozen cobwebs seemed to be hanging everywhere. Miss Haversham from *Great Expectations* was nothing compared with Mum. Hot soup and tea in front of the now roaring fire, feet in a bowl of warm water, bliss. We had no central heating or hot water system in those days so the only warm room was the sitting room with the coal fire.

Apparently, the buses from Nottingham had stopped running and Mum had had to walk home (about seven miles) after a hard day's work. Stumbling on pavement edges and walking into walls and bushes was grim, especially in the now pea-souper fog, as was bumping into the smoke-screens on the pavements; these were like braziers or large buckets containing fire and emitting smoke to fool enemy aircraft.

It was quite a blackout night for our family, but we were off to work and school again the next morning. Yes, we took it all in our stride in 1940.'

◈ A SHOWER OF INCENDIARIES ◈

'On 22nd December 1942 a bomb was dropped close to Dale Farm on Conksbury Lane, Youlgreave, followed by a shower of incendiary bombs, which it is said a German plane had left over after a raid on Sheffield. Incendiaries fell across the village, mostly at Coldwell End, two going through the roof of a bungalow and a house. The men in the area formed a chain with buckets of water and had the fires out before the fire brigade arrived. We had three incendiaries in our garden close by the window and I remember my father trying to put them out with his coat but to no avail. Fortunately the ARP man arrived and with a special tool pushed them into the soil, which of course extinguished them.

Meanwhile, my mother and I sat under a big table until we were persuaded to go across the road to a cottage with a cellar. I grabbed my dog under one arm and the budgie cage with my other hand. I remember going down the steps to this cellar, taking one look, turning round and running back up again. I felt far happier out in the open air than in that small space hewn out of solid rock. I laugh about it now, thinking how funny I must have looked with my dog and my budgie, but at the time it was very serious, for we quite expected more bombs to follow, but fortunately we were spared. I was twelve years old at the time.'

◼ LIFE IN ALFRETON ◼

'I was brought up in Alfreton during the war when the town's main industry was coal mining. I still remember the colliers trudging up our lane, black streaky faces and hands, clothes covered in coal dust, with their snap tins (tins for sandwiches to eat at break) hanging from their belts. No pit-head baths or free towels and soap in those days!

There were no cars racing up and down the lane, only the ancient pit lorry delivering free coal for the colliers, and the big black car of the pit manager, driven by Mr Twigg, his driver and handyman. The manager's wife seemed to use the car more than he did.

Although there was no television at that time, there was no shortage of entertainment, for these were the years of the heyday of the cinema, when for 1s 3d an adult and 9d a child, you could forget the blackout, food shortages and clothes coupons. There were two cinemas in Alfreton, the Empire and the Odeon, also two in nearby Somercotes. As the programmes changed twice weekly, it was possible to see a different film every night. No pictures on Sunday, until later in the war, when they were opened for the soldiers billeted in the area.

151

My mother and I went to the first house at the Empire every Friday night without fail, no matter what the film. They were all good! The Empire was cheaper and more cosy than the Odeon, which was modern and boasted shops in the foyer and a large black and white tiled vestibule. Mrs Cox's lovely sweet shop next door to the Empire supplied the customary quarter of sweets, usually Blue Bird toffees.

Although only one bomb ever fell on Alfreton, probably jettisoned from an enemy plane, but unfortunately killing the air raid warden, my Dad installed a huge rectangular shelter in our living room. We never actually used it except for playing "Houses" in. Also it was wonderful for doing jigsaws on, but very cold.

Happy days, untouched by the war when you're only eight and living far from any industrial city.'

▨ THE BLACKOUT ▨

'The blackout was a great trial in the war. "Put that light out" was the cry of the ARP warden when a chink of light showed. Darkness at night was almost total, but we did get used to it by standing still until our eyes adjusted.

Windows had to be blacked out with heavy curtains, or better still, ones lined with black fabric. This fabric was not on ration so there was no excuse for anyone to show a light. Some people made a virtue of necessity by trimming this black sateen with braid or embroidery, especially for small windows not usually curtained. A more economical way was to make a framework of laths to fit inside the frame, and nail black paper to it.

To help find the way at night we used torches. The light had to be directed to the floor and be hooded by the hand. Traffic had to have dimmed lights, inside and out. Headlights had louvred hoods. Inside the buses, the seating was changed. We sat facing each other, and most others were strap hanging. We were encouraged to wear something white to be more visible.

Moonlight was a bonus as well as being beautiful. People would boast of being able to change a sixpence by the light of the moon. Double Summer Time gave us longer daylight so saving electricity, but the farmers didn't like it as it upset the milking of the cows.'

▣ FOOD AND RATIONING ▣

'I remember going home from Sunday school the day war was declared. Mother was crying, we were very bewildered and wondered what would happen to us.

Living in the country it didn't seem to affect us much at first, but gradually the reality of it hit us – food rationing, blackout curtains and gas masks which had to be taken wherever we went, even on walks.

The time came to leave school, I did cry that day, I loved it so much. I got a job working in an office, for ten shillings a week. This firm of grocers had 17 branches. I can remember ration books very well. Each new issue had to be taken from the customers and brought to our office. The coupons were then sorted into respective kinds and sent to the Food Office, quite a mammoth task.

Saccharins came to the firm in one-stone bags. We girls took them home with little envelopes and counted them out into hundreds, the dust from them lingered in the mouth for ages. We got a halfpenny per packet at first then decided we would ask for more, and this was increased to a penny. I saved this money to pay for my holidays.

Clothing coupons were always in short supply. I can remember buying an army blanket, having it dyed a dark blue, then a dressmaker made me a coat; it was lovely and warm.'

'My father was an Income Tax Inspector, on head office relief, moving around the country. When in Nottingham, he would take sandwiches for his lunch, then join queues in the big food shops, where he would sometimes get luxuries. I remember pork pie, golden fried fish in batter, and greengages coming out of his little case.

We kept hens, and had customers rationed with us. This allowed us to buy balancer meal to feed them. Surplus eggs were traded for tea and sugar – six eggs for a quarter of tea. Black market trading was carried out with Austin Hodgkinsons on the

Market Head, Derby. They traded our eggs and chickens, we had port at Christmas, dried fruit for my brother's wedding cake, etc.

During the summer, I had to glean in the fields for grain to supplement the hens' food. We also had to collect wild rosehips to take to school for collection, to make rosehip syrup for babies. Most people kept dustpan and bucket handy. Horses meant fertiliser.

On Tuesdays, my mother met me from school and we went to Williamsons in the Wardwick, where you could have cream cakes in the cafe upstairs. They would bring you a cake stand with a set number of cakes on, and you paid for what you ate. Mum would cut one cake between us, the rest went into her bag for the men. It was the only way we could get them, as it was necessary to join the queue by 8 am to buy them over the counter.'

▣ OUR EVACUEES ▣

'Most country town had their quota of evacuees during the early war years, but Wirksworth was a little different. Ours came from London and the south but were rather larger, being heavily pregnant women who came for a short time to have their babies at Wirksworth Cottage Hospital (changed at that time to a maternity hospital). They gave a new meaning to the phrase "the streets were full" as they crammed the pavements. We ran a hardware and general shop then, in St Mary's Gate, an old property with very little space, and whenever we had a rare delivery of pots and pans or some other scarce commodity they filled the shop and overflowed like a swarm of outsize locusts, clearing the lot to the fury of our regular customers if we had no time to put any on one side. They were always glad to go back home for a "bit of life", having soon exhausted the possibilities of Wirksworth in that respect.'

▣ THEY DESERVE IT ▣

'During the war I was headmistress of the tiny school at Shottle, near Belper, where there were 22 pupils aged five to 14 years.

Soon after the war began, a searchlight unit was located in a field about 100 yards from the school. One snowy afternoon, at home time, I heard the children laughing and shouting near the camp, so I drove up to see what they were doing. They were snowballing the sentry. I sent them off on their way home.

The next morning I was told that VIPs had been visiting the camp the previous day. I talked to the children about the duties and responsibilities of a sentry on guard duty, and pointed out how naughty it was to harass and distract him. They listened attentively, but at home time there was the same noise at the camp site.

I went quickly up the hill to discover the cause. The sentry and his pals had spent their free time during the day making snowballs, and were pelting the children who, of course, were replying. When the men saw me they stopped throwing, but I wound down my car window and called, "Carry on, they deserve it", and drove away home.'

STARTING MARRIED LIFE

Young couples still wanted, perhaps with even greater urgency, to get married, and many now remember the hectic preparation and shortages that were overcome to make it a wonderful day. Separation usually followed, sometimes for years, but that was no deterrent. There were sadder stories too, though, as one GI bride remembers.

◈ THREE HECTIC WEEKS ◈

'We married on 1st September 1940, with a siren going during the ceremony but the all clear sounded too – we hoped that would be an omen for our future together. We had three hectic weeks to get the banns called, buy wedding finery and arrange a reception for 40 people. I wore a strawberry pink dress for going away with a blue coat my clever Mother had made for me but I just couldn't afford a hat so wore a length of the material in what

155

was then the new style turban. By the end of the war we hated those turbans and scarves.

Our honeymoon was spent in Kent. What a place to choose…waves of bombers to and from London and dogfights in the sky. We saw a parachute come down but had no idea if it was an English or German airman. The saddest part was travelling home by Green Line through London and seeing all the devastation, crumbling buildings, ruins still smoking, so very sad.

We had a room with my parents at first, then two rooms next door and our first little child, a daughter, Janice, was born in 1942. I had her cot right next to my bed so that if there was any bombing I could grab her quickly. One night I was so very frightened, I never knew if it was thunder, guns or bombs, the noise was horrific. We weren't bombed but houses nearby were demolished and people in the road killed by blast – the planes were jettisoning their bombs.

Our son Roger was born in 1945 and we were all sleeping in one room, so when my husband was demobbed we kept contacting all the local councillors to try and get a prefab which were just being erected in the lane where we lived. Eventually we were lucky enough to get the keys of the very first one and spent six happy years there at £1 per week. A lovely home, all mod cons, two bedrooms, bathroom, toilet, lounge and a kitchen complete with a tiny gas fridge – heaven.'

◈ NO WHITE WEDDING ◈

'On principle my father refused to allow a "white wedding" believing it to be inappropriate during wartime, but I did have a new dress and all the usual accessories. The shoes cost £3 10s, a week's wage for many people in 1940. Food rationing hadn't really begun so the reception wasn't a problem, but the war effort at Stanton by Dale could not be halted for a honeymoon! In fact Ron had been quite ill the week before the wedding and I wasn't sure until the last minute that he would make it to the church!

In the end the doctor managed to ensure Ron's appearance but the night at a hotel had to be cancelled; it was straight to the new home to be cosseted by a warm fire. As the previous owners had only just vacated the house nothing was ready and the blackout wasn't adequate so that was the first thing to be sorted out. Nothing was unpacked and I could only find one or two basins when the milkman arrived with his churn and scoop in the morning. We did have some furniture. My mother remembered the First World War and advised us to buy furniture as soon as we were engaged and store it. She knew that when war began there would be no good furniture made. She was well stocked up with tinned food by 1939; a very far-sighted lady!

By 1944 everything was rationed so when a baby arrived it was difficult to procure even the essentials. One day in Derby with my mother, I spotted a young woman carrying what I recognised as a sort of *ersatz* baby bath. It was made of papier maché and coated with some waterproof substance. I ran up to her. "Where did you find that?" I asked and on being told ran to the shop and bought the last one. Cod liver oil, rosehip syrup and orange juice (which bore little resemblance to the real thing) were available, but there were no canned baby foods. If possible I would buy a marrowbone from the butcher, simmer it for ages and combine the resultant liquor with sieved home-grown vegetables. A friend lent us a pre-war Silver Cross pram which had to be re-conditioned using rexine, the leather substitute. Later Ron made a push-chair himself, there being none in the shops.'

◼ Take Her with You ◼

'I was married to my late husband, Douglas, in July 1940 while he was on sick leave following being wounded on 10th May during a raid over Luxembourg. We were living near Uxbridge and it was rather noisy when the air raids started on London in August.

Early in September Douglas was told that he was being sent to a hospital in Matlock for recuperation. I had never heard of Matlock but he had, being a native of Leeds. Not wishing to leave me in the London area, he said to the Medical Officer, "What shall I do with my wife?" "Take her with you," he replied.

So on 16th September 1940 we set off from St Pancras. I remember the date because it was the day after the heavy air raids on London when a large number of German planes were shot down.

We arrived at Matlock station sometime during the afternoon. It was cool but fine and the colours were very beautiful. I thought it was a very pretty place but what enormous hills. (I had always lived around London and Berkshire.) We had two suitcases and Douglas said, "I expect we will have to go right to the top of that hill. That's where the hospital is bound to be." He was right. Rockside Hydro was at the top and so, although funds were scarce, we got a taxi.

The medical staff were not amused when they found the Sergeant had brought his wife along, but they agreed eventually to him helping me find somewhere to stay. This we did.

We met most afternoons for the next two months. The cinema was a treat and we walked a lot, and the weather always seemed to be fine! One day we managed to reach Smedley's Castle (now Riber Castle). I received bowling lessons in the park from some of the elderly gentlemen who were playing there. Unfortunately, I have never played since.

The Army had taken over Smedley's Hydro (now the county offices) and quite a lot of the local young men seemed to have been called up, including the husband of the lady with whom I was staying.

One evening when were were sitting listening to the wireless and knitting there was a knock on the door. It was very awkward opening doors because of the blackout and if you were not careful a light would show and the air raid warden would come calling. However we managed it, to find a young soldier from Canada on the doorstep. He said he was a cousin of my landlady and his mother had given him her address and strict instructions to call!'

◙ WE HADN'T INTENDED IT ◙

'I became a Derby resident in 1943 when, as an Air Ministry civilian clerk, I was transferred to Derby's new Council House. We bumped into the unfinished car park in an RAF van to find our office would be a huge quarter circle with large windows on the curved side. This is now a series of small offices off a curved corridor. We were keeping records of various items needed by the RAF stored at Maintenance Units around the country. It could all be done on one computer now!

As I wasn't quite 21 I didn't have full rate of pay, managing in "digs" on just over £2 per week. The landlady had 25 shillings of that.

I met Merlyn at Spondon Methodist church. He had come from Monmouthshire, sent after his chemistry degree to Celanese on work of national importance instead of the Forces. Small groups were researching a substitute for rubber (now plastics), among other things. Some of the chemicals were quite lethal.

Huge numbers of people were employed in the factory, clocking off at regular times. Many had bicycles which they rode furiously out of the factory gates, only to come to a halt at the very steep bridge over the railway and canal, to walk this distance. All except Merlyn. He was told that he went up like a tank. He had a Sturmey Archer three-speed gear which he personally had combined with a de-railleur gear with cog ratios specified to his needs. This gave him nine gears and I wonder if he was the unsung inventor of the now fashionable mountain bikes.

There were a few air raids over Spondon. One German plane brought incendiary bombs, all dropping in safe places, the sand pit, the canal, the sewage plant, etc. Perhaps the bombers following them had no markers, thus missing their factory target.

We hadn't really intended getting married as early as we did, but came across a woman who wanted to let her house, furnished, and go working on the land. It was essential that she and the young son should go as soon as possible. There was absolutely no thought that we should move in, perhaps getting married later. Both families were a bit dumb-struck but my mother rallied round arranging for a wedding cake – no icing, but a cardboard cover over a rich as possible fruit cake.

We found that the so-called furnished house was actually very uncomfortable and embarrassing apartments, with various American soldier "uncles" coming to stay the night with the landlady. We soon moved out and were taken in by kindly people.

Our bed, sent by rail, came from my parents. Other furniture was secondhand as nothing new was being produced, everything being diverted to the war effort. So we progressed until we had a house of our own and by that time, the beginnings of our family.'

❈ I BECAME A GI BRIDE ❈

'Four days after my 16th birthday Hank and I were married – that is, we entered the Register Office by the back door and emerged four minutes later from the front door as man and wife. A short time later I found myself boarding the *Queen Mary* to cross the Atlantic – not long before I had not been allowed to cross town.

My story started on VE Day. . .or perhaps a little before. We had been expecting the end of hostilities to be announced for some days before it actually was, and this enabled many of us to plan some celebrations. I was evacuated during the war to a boarding school not far from here. This school, by error or design, was flanked on one side by a German POW camp and on the other by a US Air Force base. The girls from our school, and I was amongst them, lost no time in making the acquaintance of members from either camp! Needless to say our end of war celebrations were to include members of this mini "United Nations".

My best friend "Bubbles", also an evacuee, was visited on this day by her father who very kindly obtained permission for us to go into the nearby town – where we enjoyed a memorable meal and later saw a film of George Formby enlisting in the army (a bit late), but I remember the earth-shattering applause when the film stopped and the announcement was made: "Hitler is defeated". We returned to school at the regulation hour of 8 pm, but no sooner had our chaperone departed than we ourselves left once more by the rear exit – this time to meet up with Hans and

Hank and to return to the bright lights and all the action. We had a marvellous evening, each of us returning to our respective camps via some gap in the hedge or over some forbidden fence. We crept silently into the dormitory confident that we had been seen by no one.

However, this was not the case, and next day our whole world fell apart when Bubbles and I were summoned to the headmaster's office, to explain the headlines on the local evening paper. It seems some hapless reporter keen to get a story had, quite unknown to us, snapped us in a very unladylike pose together with our escorts.

To say that the headmaster was incensed would be an understatement. The fact that our liaisons had been going on for some time we thought might lessen the severity of his disapproval, but quite the reverse. That this sort of thing had been going on and right under his nose so to speak was a matter that could only be dealt with by our immediate expulsion, and we left school that very day. I was returned home in disgrace. My mother was crying – my father said what else did you expect? My mother decided the only solution was that I be married as soon as legally possible, my father said it was the best we could make of a bad job. The day before I was to be married is a day I shall never forget as long as I live.

My mother called me into what was known as the front room, a room which housed all the best furniture, was kept locked and only opened on very special occasions. I was conscious of the gravity of the interview. The doors were closed, the curtains drawn and my mother took her keys and moved slowly over to the metal box where she kept items of value and important documents. She removed some old photos and papers, then with great difficulty started to talk round a subject, in the way that only parents of those days knew how!

I was about to put her out of her dilemma by announcing that I already knew all about the birds and the bees when she stopped me abruptly by announcing: "My child – you are not my child, you came as a visitor to this house, and you have stayed for 16 years. Your name is not what you think it is, your name is Foundling. We have cared for you for all these years and you have disgraced us as your mother disgraced her mother." (Not true – but she thought so.)

I gaped at my mother, was she off her head? Out of her mind? Was I really hearing these words or was it all a bad dream? That night sleep would not come to me. When I got up my father could not look at me, the younger members of the family, aware that all was not well, were being unnaturally kind to me, at the same time bartering between them who would now sleep in my bed. I still do not know how I got through those hours leading up to what was supposed to be "the happiest day of my life". But the time finally arrived and I entered the "Palace of Weddings" where Hank, accompanied by Hans and Bubbles, was to make an honest woman of me. He did not flinch or show any emotion or surprise when he heard the name of the schoolgirl he was to take into unholy matrimony.

We embarked on the *Queen Mary* in company with many other brides – but I must have been the only bride on board to have changed her name three times in 24 hours!

That this marriage lasted for over five years was to the credit of the two stars – and its beginning was in no way responsible for its end. But that, reader, is another story.

This is a Second World War story, although you could be forgiven for thinking the characters belonged to the First.'

———

DOING OUR BIT

In the armed services or on the Home Front, we all did our bit for the war effort. The Home Guard, the Women's Land Army, munitions factories, hospitals and the railways were just some of the essential areas in which we worked.

▣ CONSCRIPTED TO WORK ▣

'Although thousands of women and girls worked in munitions, not many had to work in the operating department on the railways. I was conscripted to work in a signal box.

Small boxes were usually in remote places so it was a very lonely life, and we often had to work twelve hour shifts, alternate days and nights. We had a small air raid shelter inside the box and the windows were taped to stop flying glass in the event of an explosion. The lighting was a paraffin lamp over the desk with a tin shade to give a small light to do the bookwork.'

'Charlesworth had evacuees from Manchester, Lowestoft, and even German children. One woman from Lowestoft – Vera Osborne – brought her netting skills from the fishing town to the village. William Edwards & Son owned a factory and camouflage nets were made there, and also huge heavy steel nets for the Navy (for snaring submarines). Eight young women worked on each net and as they worked the men threw the heavy netting over poles to take the weight. Government inspectors came every week to inspect this essential war work. The girls were paid high wages, working twelve hours a day six days a week. The factory also made tagging for steel helmet lacings, and lanyards among other items.'

✹ ON MUNITIONS ✹

'I was a young teenager and still at school when war broke out in 1939. I lived on a farm at Darley Moor. Shortly after the outbreak of war, two nearby farms were requisitioned, along with the "Hollywood" where we used to play. An aerodrome was built on Darley Moor, and military huts on some of our fields. We were supplied with an indoor air-raid shelter, in case of enemy action. This had a steel top to be used as a dining table, and we civilians could go underneath for protection. The aerodrome was not used a great deal, but a bomber crashed there one night, only a quarter of a mile from our house, and all lives were lost. I can still remember the smell of the foam used to put out the fire.

In 1942 I was "called up" to work on munitions – Rolls-Royce had taken over the corset factory in Ashbourne. The horror the first morning I arrived. I stood at the top of the stairs, and there were machines as far as I could see, driven by belts whizzing down from the ceiling. The noise was deafening, and this was where I worked, two weeks on days and two weeks on nights, for the next three years. The machine I was put on made tappet screws. Hot oil running over hot steel would spit out at me, along with all the turnings. The smell was revolting. I wore old shoes, and overalls made from blackout material. After a few weeks on this machine I was promoted to Inspection. I had to fetch two specimens from each machine and make sure the dimensions were correct.

I met some lovely people there; we had music when we worked on nights, and danced in the tea breaks. There was a canteen with very little choice – nearly always baked beans on toast. When on nights I worked six nights a week, 7.30 pm to 6.30 am, for £6 a week. On one night a week we could clock in at 9 pm.

I cycled to work in the blackout. My father hated me cycling in the dark – he would get quite upset and then I would cry all the way to Ashbourne. It was really creepy cycling home at 6.30 on dark mornings, things rustled in the hedgerows, and when it was moonlight there were shadows everywhere. Some of the men on the shop floor would try to frighten me by saying a man had escaped from the prisoner of war camp at Sudbury.

I was working on the shop floor the morning in November 1944 when there was a huge explosion at the munitions dump at Fauld. The belts working the machines stopped for an instant, but we were not to know the reason until much later. Many lives were lost and homes disappeared. The crater still exists, and every year a memorial service is held.'

❖ EVERYONE DID THEIR BIT ❖

'When war was declared my father became an air raid warden. Then the siren sounded he had to patrol from our house in Breadsall to the next village, presumably to look out for enemy parachutists. My brother and I were always relieved to hear his returning footsteps. We were used to the blackout as we did not have street lighting.

One day an army regiment came to do a "mock battle exercise" in the woods opposite our house. During the exercise three soldiers came to our house to ask if my mother would make them some tea. Of course, Mother willingly did so but a short time later an officer came and reprimanded my mother in severe terms for making tea for "the enemy".

Two ladies who lived at Church House in the village were WI members and taught our mother how to use meagre rations to make nourishing meals and the canning and bottling of fruit. A butcher from Ripley delivered meat pies to the village once a fortnight, and these were eagerly awaited as a treat to supplement rations.

I remember being a "victim" in a First Aid exercise. We were taken to a remote field with a label pinned to our clothes saying what injuries we had sustained. We were then taken by ambulance to the First Aid Post and swathed in bandages. The Home Guard were a smart troop and we watched them parade through the village. Everyone seemed to do their bit for the war effort, purchasing National Savings Certificates, digging for victory and "make do and mend".

VE Day came with rejoicing that the war in Europe was over. The church bells were rung after being silent in the war years. My mother opened our house for all our neighbours to celebrate peace. We had nothing very much in the way of refreshments, just a great sing-a-long with the piano and the joy of being together.'

'The Observer Corps was formed in 1938, mainly from people who had served in the First World War and were too old to serve again. The first headquarters was below the telephone exchange in Becket Street, Derby. It was later moved to a building behind the Broadway Hotel on the Duffield Road.

An ARP headquarters was at The Grange at Littleover. There were five manned posts. ARP messengers (aged 13 to 16 years) took urgent messages on their bicycles from The Grange to various sub-stations. The Littleover air raid siren was on the roof of The Grange.'

'Before the war I attended Wirksworth grammar school with my brother. We walked there and back each day because we were not allowed bicycles, these being considered too dangerous on the hills. On one occasion in 1936 I turned the corner on Wirksworth Moor and met a group of young Germans; they were marching and dressed in brown shirts with swastikas on their armbands. They were from a summer school which was situated in the big wood in Alderwasley, and I imagine that they were going into Wirksworth to buy their provisions. Later on, during the war, the occupants of this camp were rounded up by the Home Guard and detained until the end of the war. Apparently they had been signalling to enemy aircraft.

During the early months of the war my father belonged to the Local Defence Volunteers and wore an armband with the initials LDV. He went on duty one night carrying a pitchfork and spent the night sitting up a tree guarding the wireworks at Ambergate. By this time he must have been in his late sixties. Later on they were issued with uniform and firearms and were called the Home Guard.

In 1940 I was nursing at the Children's Hospital in Derby and if there was an air raid we had to move all the cots into the centre of the ward. One evening a bomb dropped near to the hospital and the electric power was cut off. Some of the windows near the operating theatre were broken and an operation was in progress, so we had to hold up blackout to the windows. A generator was brought in to provide the electricity. The matron of the hospital at this time was rather frail and could not cope with air raids, she used to pass out and on one occasion we had to push her under a knee-hole desk in the ward for protection, not forgetting her tin hat.

I remember knitting a balaclava helmet for navy personnel, having collected the wool which was free from the Gaumont cinema in Derby.'

▣ IN THE HOME GUARD ▣

'Each time I see the programme *Dad's Army* on the television it brings back the many happy hours I had serving with the Home Guard in Whaley Bridge. Six friends and myself had gone through Guides together, then graduated to Rangers and when we had outgrown that we were invited to join the Home Guard. I am sure that our Captain was the model for the television series. He strutted around with a stick under his arm, referred to us as "the gels" and, like Captain Mainwaring, he took his duties very seriously indeed.

We were installed in an office in Market Street, fitted out with a uniform of khaki drill battledress top and skirt and wore our navy blue Ranger berets with a Home Guard badge on the front. We practised our morse code on a buzzer and semaphore with flags, and also learned how to take messages on the telephone. I was the telephonist most of the time and all messages had to be written out in triplicate, one copy for the office file, one sent to HQ and what happened to the third copy is perhaps best forgotten.

One Sunday we were informed that we were going to be attacked by the Pioneer Corps, based in Buxton, and all battle stations had to be manned from nine o'clock onwards. Great excitement! Messages were sent and received and we were kept very busy indeed. Suddenly the office door burst open and we were told by a very excited Captain that the enemy were approaching and the "gels" would have to be evacuated through the window by the use of ropes and lowered down at the rear of the premises into the river below. Now, that river was all of 40 feet away and we didn't really think much of the idea at all. The office sergeant didn't either because I distinctly remember him saying "Not likely", or words to that effect.

Anyway, we gathered together our equipment and sprinted through the front door, making our way down Market Street to our temporary office at a local mill. As we left the building we saw a figure across the road lounging on the steps of the Mechanics Institute. I think he was in disguise because his face was blackened and around his helmet he had a wreath of laurel leaves; a cigarette hung from his mouth and he carried a rifle. We did not know whether he was the enemy or not so we waved in a friendly manner and called "Hello". He responded with a wink and pointed his rifle at us so we ran faster than ever, not wishing to be taken prisoner. After a time a whistle sounded, the battle was over and we all went home to Sunday lunch. We had lost.

We were also sent on manoeuvres occasionally on Taxal Moor, and I had to man a field telephone. This never worked and it was impossible either to take messages or receive them so there was nothing for it but to call in the services of the despatch riders. One was the manager in the office at my place of employment so I leapt on the pillion seat of his bike and had a ride down to HQ. Very daring in those days, but exceedingly uncomfortable as I burned my leg on his exhaust pipe. My mother was not impressed, in fact she didn't think much of the whole idea of girls in the Home Guard, but I told her there was a war on (as if she didn't know) and I went anyway.

Eventually the war was over and we were all stood down, marching past the bigwigs in the Crescent in Buxton, and it was time to think of other things. Boys were coming back from the Forces. There was some serious courting to be done and thoughts of marriage. Still, while it lasted it was a time to look back on and have a good laugh at our antics.'

▣ WITH THE ROYAL SIGNALS ◈

'We first saw Kedleston from the back of an army troop carrier on a pouring wet evening in May 1943. What we didn't know was that those wooden huts under the dripping trees were to be our home for the next 18 months.

We had trained in Douglas as wireless operators and now were to work shifts round the clock, intercepting morse signals from enemy forces on the continent, in the Operations Block. There was a large set room, teleprinters' room which was always busy and very noisy, sending intercepted traffic to Bletchley Park, and a rest room where we had curled jam sandwiches and very thick strong cocoa on night shift breaks.

The mess, cookhouse and NAAFI were alongside the road from the Hall to the present car park and we paraded for work outside the mess to march up to the "Ops Block". Company Office was in the Hall, an oak panelled room behind the kitchen where the bikes were kept.

Off duty we planted potatoes in May and harvested them in October, played tennis on the courts in front of the Hall and hockey in the park, had PT, dug the garden and planted flowers round the hut and cycled all round the Derbyshire countryside. There were various craft classes, orderly duties and lectures on

HRH Princess Mary inspecting 'D' Watch of No 4 Company ATS Royal Signals, Kedleston Hall in 1943.

current affairs, church parade on Sunday morning, the service in the lovely old church being conducted by Rev Leake. HRH Princess Mary, the Princess Royal visited the camp. We had occasional air raid practice, diving into the ha-ha round the Hall gardens which doubled as an air raid shelter.

On 6th June 1944, when we came off night shift at seven o'clock the clear blue sky was full of planes and the noise of their engines filled the air. When we woke in the afternoon there was a note pinned to each bed which said our troops had this morning invaded France and the Second Front had begun. The huge map of Europe on the set room wall showed our troops' advance across northern France and sometimes an operator would intercept frantic signals from her wireless set followed by plain language and then silence.

Bus services into Derby were almost non-existent but we managed to get lifts occasionally, otherwise it was a long walk to the trolley bus terminus outside the Markeaton Hotel. We queued for the "gods" at the Grand Theatre, had tea at the Picture House with its huge coal fire in the hall, and the Gaumont, Coliseum, Regal and Hippodrome were just a few of the places where we would be warm and dry as a change from the chilly conditions in camp.'

❖ IN THE HOSPITALS ❖

'I never really wanted to be a nurse. It was 1943 and, unknown to my parents, I tried to enlist in the Wrens to "do my bit" but they didn't want me! Following this I noticed an advertisement in the newspaper: "Why not make Nursing your career?" "Why not?" I thought. "Anything for a spot of excitement." My parents weren't very keen on the idea but eventually agreed and later Mum accompanied me to Birmingham where I had been accepted as a Probationer Nurse at the Birmingham Accident Hospital.

I must confess to a tear glistening as I said goodbye to Mum outside the hospital. After the peace and quiet of Breadsall, as it then was, I thought I would never sleep with trams clanking past the front of the hospital and trains shunting and canal barges chugging past the side. However, I soon became used to it and was quickly swept up into the busy hubbub of hospital life and ensconced in PTS (Preliminary Training School) for three months' initial training.

I had no idea how much domestic work would be involved like sink cleaning (we used Gospo for this) and polishing: "Use some elbow grease, Nurse!" Before we swept the floors, we had to scatter wet tea leaves down to lay the dust!

Numerous lectures taught us the names of all the bones, muscles, nerves etc in the body; our heads were spinning at the end of the day. Interspersed with these were practical sessions where we learned the various arts of bed making, bandaging, taking temperatures and inserting awful "Ryles tubes" into the stomach via the nose (with much heaving!). We even saw how

170

leeches were used to bleed people. This was done on a piece of raw liver which was *not* a pretty sight. Occasionally we were let loose on the wards for a while to "do it for real".

Three months later, feeling very proud of ourselves, we were delegated to a ward and soon became immersed. We started getting convoys in from the war zones. Wounded, dirty and exhausted men, but still, incredibly, smiling and *so* glad to be back home. One of our first convoys was from the debacle that was Arnhem and we also had many burns patients from men trapped in blazing tanks.

A new specialised Burns Unit was set up at the hospital by Colonel Leonard Colebrook and I was greatly privileged to have been part of its opening team. They did a wonderful job and quickly gained fame from their new techniques. This was the time of the advent of penicillin and we made our own in the pathology laboratory. In those days, treatment consisted of massive, three hourly, intramuscular injections which now seems horrific. However, it really worked and seeing those brave young men recovering so well was great.

Memories, sad and happy times and especially togetherness, and all for £3 a month starting pay and £5 when I qualified at the Queen Elizabeth Hospital four years later!'

'In 1944 I was working at the Derby Royal Infirmary. We had to be in by 11 pm, the door was locked then. There was a certain window on the ground floor which could be pushed open, the unfortunate occupant being wakened by bodies scrambling through the windows, probably pushed through by their boyfriends. The fire escape door was accidently left open sometimes!

The first ward I worked on had 35 beds occupied by soldiers. Three wards in the DRI were taken over by the armed forces, wounded during the fighting in Europe after D-Day. They arrived in convoys from hospital trains met at Derby station by the ambulances, usually at 3 am. All day staff were recalled to the wards to admit the men and get them into bed, and the theatres worked at night and the next day as many needed surgery. Some had lost limbs, others had complicated fractures or were badly wounded.

When they started to recover they were very high spirited and broke all the rules, but we turned a blind eye. The public in Derby were very generous. They brought food parcels in and concert parties came to entertain on the ward. The men that could go out on crutches or in wheelchairs were taken out to parties. The Carriage & Wagon works, Rolls-Royce and many other factories were very generous in visiting and providing gifts.

Ward 8 was the officers' ward. When mobile they used to go out at night on crutches or others walking. They came in late at night a little the worse for wear, noisy and singing and we had to persuade them to go to bed before night sister came round.'

⊡ ENGINE DRIVER WITH THE LMS ⊡

'My father was an engine driver with the old London, Midland and Scottish Railways for 40 years. During the war the hours he had to work were unpredictable and he would sometimes be away from home for 18 hours with only a sandwich and a bottle of cold tea to sustain him.

One night he took a goods train to York where an air raid was in progress. Knowing that his train carried ammunition he decided that the safest thing to do was to contact the signalman and then take the train back again, which he did! I also remember the "knocker up". As work times were different each day, a man was employed to come and knock on doors to wake the men up. I would be disturbed by him saying, 'Alton, Alton, 3.30 am train to Wellingborough," or whatever the destination was. He wouldn't leave until he was answered.'

⊡ THE WOMEN'S LAND ARMY ⊡

'When the war began in 1939, young men and women at the age of 17 years were called into the Armed Forces. Miners and farm workers were exempt from the call up. An alternative to the Forces was to work in a munitions factory but I chose to join the Women's Land Army.

This army of young women valiantly took the place of absent

172

men from farms, horticulture or forestry. They came from all walks of life. So on 6th March 1944, I became an enrolled member of the WLA, and was scheduled to work in dairy and arable farming, which was my choice.

My uniform duly arrived at my home. It consisted of a dark beige, knee length overcoat, beige felt hat with badge, beige Aertex working shirts, one beige cotton dress shirt, two green wool V-necked jumpers, two pairs of khaki knee breeches, three pairs of beige knee high wool socks, two khaki cotton twill dungarees, two long sleeved knee length cotton twill overalls with detachable buttons, one pair of wellingtons with a thick tread, one pair of very stiff leather ankle boots, one pair of very hard leather walking shoes with steel heel caps, one green tie and green armband with a red crown embroidered on it.'

'My time in the Land Army started when I was 17. On joining I was sent to a fruit farm where I was put on spraying fruit trees. This was done with a nicotine solution which made your hair, eyebrows and nails turn yellow.

Then I began general farming. Our day started at 6.30 am with breakfast, and then at 7 am we all piled into a coal lorry to be dropped at our various farms within about a 20 mile radius. Those who were sent to farms close at hand cycled there. We were issued with billycans with our lunch which consisted of a few sandwiches, a slice of cake, and maybe an apple, which we invariably ate in a field or in bad weather hopefully we would find a barn. We returned about 6.30 pm when it was a mad rush to beat everyone to the bathroom (I'm afraid all modesty went out of the window).

Five of us followed a threshing drum around to different farms for six months, threshing every day. This was quite a tiring job and also dirty; we did bond cutting, feeding the sheaves into the drum and clearing the chaff away, which if not kept down could soon be as high as yourself. When we came to the bottom of the rick we wired it off and then had to tuck our dungarees in our socks and with our pitchforks had to kill the mice, not a pleasant job.

We sometimes worked with German and Italian prisoners of war, who on the whole weren't too bad; the Germans I found hard working but the Italians tended to be lazy, but they didn't give us any trouble.

We did a variety of jobs, potato planting, picking and sorting, picking and loading sugar beet, cleaning pigsties, milking etc. The lorry picked us up about 6 pm, a tired and dirty bunch of girls but after a bath and a meal we were ready to go out for our evening entertainment, or stop in and listen to the wireless and write letters.'

'In June 1944 I was married to my Air Force boyfriend. To our surprise when we came out of the church the land girls had formed a guard of honour of pitchforks for me.

It was April 1946 that I knew I was going to have a baby, so of course I had to finish work. I put my uniform and other LA clothes into a suitcase and went to the WLA Headquarters to hand them in. I was allowed to keep my two shirts, shoes, sweater and hat badge. The lady in the office said they were very pleased with my report from my two employers. They had both reported that I had been an excellent worker and as good as any of the men. The lady shook hands with me and said I had done an excellent job for my country and thanked me very much. I was then handed a letter from the Queen Mother. I came home on the train feeling satisfied that I had done my "bit" for my country. I had now to start a new kind of life, looking after my husband and children.'

A Child's War

The war brought excitement, terror and new people into many children's lives, whether at home or as evacuees in the villages. It left indelible impressions on those who were young during those years.

◈ THE BEGINNING ◈

'I was ten in 1938, crisis year. Trenches were built on our local "rec". We children were warned to keep out, but unfortunately one boy was killed when a trench caved in. After that they were all filled in.

I was in chapel on Sunday morning, 3rd September 1939, when at 11 am a church steward came in and whispered the news. "Go straight home," we were told. Mum was in the garden talking to our neighbour. "Nine days' wonder," they were saying. "All will be over by Christmas!" Which Christmas?

Soon after, a man came to our door to register everyone for identity cards. I shall never forget our family's numbers. Over the wall next door, Ann and William Green, our neighbours, gave him their names, to which we heard the man say, "Ah! Green Annie and Green Willie." This name, affectionately, stuck for years. Being fitted for gas masks was another trial. The smell of the things was horrible, you had to practise wearing it and taking it on and off. My six year old sister wasn't having anything to do with this, she screamed and kicked and was altogether terrified. Trying a Mickey Mouse mask was suggested, but that frightened her more so she had an ordinary one.

Gas masks were given to us in cardboard boxes, soon to be changed to tin boxes. Standing in line at school, there was always a gas mask inspection, but woe betide anyone who rattled their gas mask tin against their partner's as they went into class. Later we had posh black leather cases, like handbags. You took it everywhere. Sometimes there was smoked gas practice, we had to wear our masks and walk through the smoke, but fortunately we never had to face the real thing.

In the beginning a pupil had to stand sentry duty outside the class ready to call "Scatter" if the sirens sounded. We seemed to spend a lot of time practising the quick evacuation to the school shelter, always dark and damp with wet floors. I can remember one girl having a hysterical fit. Teacher always started the singing with *South of the Border* to keep spirits up.

We didn't get Anderson shelters in our street, but brick ones built above the ground on the road. These always seemed to be locked. Most people on our street slept in their cellars. Ours was well equipped with mattress and bedding. I suppose it was fun until the novelty wore off. Then a bed was put into the front parlour, leaving easy access to the cellar and the front door.

The night five bombs were dropped landing in the fields at the bottom of the street, we were upstairs in bed, having been lulled into a false sense of security. The house shook, windows shattered, ARP wardens were racing up and down the street blowing whistles and shouting. Grandad came rushing to our house to check that we were OK, he had lost his windows and greenhouse. Next morning we all went to see the bomb craters, not as big as I had expected. Had to go to school in the afternoon. Disappointing!'

▣ EVACUEES AND SCHOOL ▣

'Since we were fairly safe at Stanton by Dale, evacuees from London were billeted in the area and attended our large village school. We were told prior to their arrival that they came from London and had experienced dreadful events due to the bombing. We were not to mention aeroplanes or ask them anything about their lives in London as such questions would bring back distressing memories. Unfortunately these well-meant instructions had the effect of making us frightfully curious as to how the evacuees would react in such circumstances. Would they scream and cry? Would they fall on the floor in fits? We were dying to know. Imagine our

176

Pentrich schoolchildren in 1940. Many school rolls were swelled by evacuees.

disappointment when some of the boys started bragging about their knowledge of the different types of aeroplane and running about, arms outstretched, making engine noises and imitating the *crump* of bombs hitting buildings. What a let down, no hysterics, no fits.

I started school on my fifth birthday in 1941 and my mother must have been very glad since I had plagued the life out of her during the last year or two being bored at home and absolutely dying to get to school. However, after only a week I went down with a fairly mild dose of whooping cough and so there was no more school until the new term began in September when to my disgust I was put back into the "baby class". I had thought I would be "put up" despite only having the one week and I was very miffed. There were between 48 and 52 children in my class all the way up that school and all the teachers were women except for one man who I think must have been invalided out of the forces during the war.

Every now and then the air raid siren would sound and we

would be ushered in neat lines across the playground to the deep shelters. We never knew if there was a real alarm because the teachers always said it was a "practice", but it was a great diversion which most of us enjoyed. We had to climb down a hole on vertical ladders into the dark; a teacher would be at the bottom to direct us to our seats which were slatted wooden benches placed along the walls of narrow passages. Some children were afraid of the dark and would cry and so they sat on teacher's knee. When we were all down and accounted for on the register, torches were switched off and we sat in the dark. "Miss" organised clapping and singing games until it was time to emerge blinking into daylight again.

On the way home from school we would amuse ourselves by chalking German swastikas on the pavements and then scare ourselves wondering what would happen to us if the police found out what we'd done. By the age of eight or nine some of us really did begin to wonder what would happen if the Germans invaded and we longed for the war to be over, provided that we won.'

✦ MEMORIES OF MICKLEOVER ✦

'We had an indoor shelter of railway sleepers, with a slate-bed billiard table on the top. When we slept in the shelter, we would listen for the guns. We had a name for each one, not the recognised ones but our own version. Our Big Bertha was on the racecourse. It was involved in a daylight episode that I remember vividly. I went into the garden to play on my swing. I heard a plane, recognised the sound as a German one, started to look up, and he was so low he took a piece off the top of the shed. I saw the pilot's face, surrounded by a leather helmet. He was looking straight at me. I still see his face in my nightmares. Although he was hedgehopping to avoid the guns, he was, I believe shot down over the racecourse.

The school had no shelter – it was under your desk, with your gas mask at the ready, or run for home if there seemed to be time. When the explosion occurred at Fauld, the building shook. We didn't wait to be told. Under our desks we went, but we were soon out, standing on the pipes to watch the army lorries and fire engines going along Uttoxeter Road.

My father was a keen gardener – the lawns kept shrinking as he dug for victory. Behind our front hedge was a row of marguerite daisies, very large and very white. We had a visit from an air raid warden, asking Dad to cover them up at night, as they were visible from the air and were being used as a marker by the bombers.'

◈ BOMBS AND SOLDIERS ◈

'I remember the night in 1940 when the bombs were dropped. We were in our neighbour's air raid shelter at Woodthorpe. I thought the top of our house must have been blown off because the noise was so great. In fact, it was a land-mine and it destroyed Duckmanton school a few miles away. The next attack was much closer to home and actually blew all the windows and ceilings down in our house and damaged the Mastin Moor hospital nearby. We hadn't visited the shelter that night and I slept through it all! It was very exciting and scary and we were able to have a day off school.

I also remember folding my clothes in neat order so that they could be donned quickly in case Hitler came during the night. I was scared of any men in long overcoats and trilby hats – they were sure to be spies and should be avoided at all costs.

We only attended school for part of the day for a time because soldiers were billeted there. On one occasion the troops were very generous with oranges and chocolate and even allowed me to inspect the inside of a tank. My identity number was engraved on my heart as well as on a bracelet and I can still recall the smell of my gas mask and the awful claustrophobia when I practised wearing it. These memories and many more will never fade. I was seven years old at this time.'

◈ PERFUMED PERIL ◈

'Even as a very young lady, aged four, in the early days of the war, I was extremely fond of perfume! A kind young neighbour, knowing my passion, saved me all her perfume bottles with the

179

last few precious drops of "Evening in Paris", "Californian Poppy", and, best of all "Phul-Nana", my favourite, with a seductive dancing girl swathed in pink robes pictured on the label.

One particular evening, the sirens sounded their warning too late for us to make our usual orderly exodus to the air raid shelter in the garden, before we heard the distinctive sound of enemy aircraft overhead.

The pantry (under the stairs) was our emergency bolt hole, where we packed in like sardines, praying that it wouldn't last too long. There were several of us, including my uncle who was then a young soldier home on leave, all sitting amongst the pickling jars, ironing board and multifarious items. As you can imagine, it rapidly became stuffy, the atmosphere not being improved by the fact that I had with me, along with several teddy bears and a couple of dolls, a bottle of "Californian Poppy" rather fuller than usual, which I shared generously between the teddies and family alike.

Apparently, my uncle stoically suffered this overpowering aroma for some time, but eventually, with a despairing cry of, "Bombs, or no ruddy bombs, I'm getting out of here", he bolted for the comparative fresh air of the backyard, despite the air raid which was still raging overhead.

The next morning, my mother found by the back door an enormous piece of shrapnel, which occupied pride of place in the glass cabinet for many years.

Thank goodness it missed him, but not surprisingly, "Californian Poppy" didn't seem to be very popular with our family after that!'

❖ NOT HOW TO BEHAVE ❖

'We lived in Willington from early 1940. I used to ride my bicycle all around the local lanes and villages. One day I had gone up Castleway Lane and over the A38 towards Egginton Junction and on the way back I was overtaken by a truck full of American soldiers. I picked up the oranges which they threw out and took them home with glee. My mother was not at all amused by the incident and I was given a lecture on how a well brought up young lady should behave. I never knew what became of the oranges.'

◙ TIME OFF FOR PICKING ◙

'At Baslow school we had afternoons out to collect blackberries
and rosehips for syrup towards the war effort. We invaded Yeld
Wood and the edge of the moors for those with Mr Sheldon the
headmaster. Time was allowed out of school for back-breaking
potato picking, which was quite remunerative.'

◙ GROWING UP FAST ◙

'When war broke out, in 1939, I was 14 years old. I was the elder
daughter of a miner in one of those scruffy nondescript towns
which sprawl northwards through the Erewash valley, plotting
the path of the Industrial Revolution through the area. We lived
on a council estate surrounded by kindly women and hard-
drinking men, in a close community with no comprehension of
the upheaval which was to come.

Some six years earlier my mother had died leaving my father the
unenviable task of bringing up two young girls alone. He was ill-
prepared for the role which had been cast for him. He was a quiet
uncomplicated man, face to face with the problem of survival. He
did his best and we did survive in a rough and ready way.

We grew up fast in that first long winter of the war. We grew
accustomed to change, to food shortages, to queues and the
blackout; above all to the misery of the blackout.

With the descent of night the blackness was pervasive.
Cocooned in its mystery we relied more on sound and memory
than on sight. Shrouded vehicle lights cast an eerie beam from
their slotted cowls peering just a few feet ahead in the darkness.
Few ventured out without good reason; the unwilling night shift
on their way to work, the eager dayshift in search of a pub that
might have some beer or cigarettes, Both beer and cigarettes
were in short supply as was good humour on those dark nights
with people stumbling on their way, cursing in frustration as
they went, banging and barging into lamp-posts and slithering
from the edges of pavements.

The days passed, the war dragged on until one fateful night some years later I was met on the doorstep by a nervous neighbour. Ill at ease, he explained to me that my father had been taken to hospital following an accident. I was to visit him without delay.

He had been struck down by a bus in the centre of town. Being somewhat deaf, he neither heard nor saw the bus in the darkness – another victim of the blackout.

That same night he died and so did my familiar world. I felt alone and afraid. My journey into an uncertain future had begun.'

◈ WAITING FOR THE DUST TO SETTLE ◈

'My recollections of the war are somewhat spasmodic, rather hazy, but nevertheless real. I was attending Nightingale Road junior school in Derby when the war began, later going to Allenton secondary modern. My elder sister and myself lived with our parents at 100 Hawthorn Street which is within yards of Rolls-Royce, this made it convenient for my father who worked there but was considered dangerous from the point of view of air raids. When, however, inevitably the chance came for me to be evacuated to the safer surroundings of the countryside I told my mother I did not want to go. This was probably a mistake but as a child you have no sense of mortality and being of a shy disposition I did not relish the thought of leaving home for some "distant land".

I recall some nights being roused by the sound of air raid sirens and half asleep descending into the damp, dank depths of next door's Anderson shelter, usually only to sit there for a while before the welcoming sound of the all clear broke the silence. Ironically, the time when my parents and I were in the most danger came with no forewarning siren. Picture the scene: my sister had left for work, I had just risen from bed, my father was mixing bread and milk on the kitchen table for his canaries, my mother was around too, when out of the murky sky a lone raider struck. There were a few preliminary bursts of anti-aircraft fire, our eyes met and as one we fled to the front room and the relative "safety" of the indoor Morrison shelter. As I recall I was the last to get in and did so to the accompaniment of aircraft noises and a chorus of explosions. Afterwards the silence was profound. I think my mother broke it with the words, "The windows are in." This to me was incredible. This lone raider could easily have killed us but I thought it unbelievable that he should dare to break our windows. It took a while for the dust to settle around the street, both literally and metaphorically and our family spent the next few days sleeping at an aunt's on Harvey Road. A detached house on the corner not 50 yards away from us suffered a direct hit and was flattened but by some great good fortune the family were away at the time. Sadly, however, a young boy some seven houses away was killed.

During the rest of the war the full scale blitz which was expected to take place on Rolls-Royce did not materialise, if it had I probably would not be writing this now.'

◙ THE LONG WALK HOME ◙

'War became a reality for me on the Sunday before Christmas 1940. I was eleven years old and we'd been visiting Grandma who lived at Barlborough. My parents, younger sister and I were heading for the bus home when the air raid siren wailed. There were no buses during air raids so we had to walk the six miles home to Poolsbrook.

It was one of those clear frosty moonlit nights when you could see for miles, especially as the road was built along a high ridge. We could hear the enemy aircraft passing overhead as they sped on their way to attack Sheffield on our right just over the horizon.

The sky was dull red at first but soon it was glowing with bright fiery splashes. This was Sheffield and its suburbs ablaze. We stood watching for about an hour – our Mum wasn't too pleased, she wanted us home and in our beds.

At one point over to our left towards Bolsover and Duckmanton, we saw a strange shadowy object which seemed to be floating downwards in the still night air. We were convinced it was a German pilot bailing out of a damaged aircraft. We finally arrived home at 2 am and Mum bundled us off to bed as soon as the all clear signal sounded.

8th June, 1946

To-day, as we celebrate victory, I send this personal message to you and all other boys and girls at school. For you have shared in the hardships and dangers of a total war and you have shared no less in the triumph of the Allied Nations.

I know you will always feel proud to belong to a country which was capable of such supreme effort; proud, too, of parents and elder brothers and sisters who by their courage, endurance and enterprise brought victory. May these qualities be yours as you grow up and join in the common effort to establish among the nations of the world unity and peace.

George R.I.

The VE Day message sent to schoolchildren by King George.

Next morning, I was up as usual at 7 am ready for the mile and a half walk over the fields to my school at Duckmanton. However, Dad said there would be no classes that day because the school had been damaged by a parachute land-mine. Possibly that was the mystery object we'd seen last night. I insisted that I really should go to school. (Well I wanted to see the damage for myself.)

The school was a series of single storey wooden buildings and apparently the parachute attached to the land-mine had become entangled in a tree behind the Science Building. It remained suspended for a while but when the branch snapped the mine exploded on impact, demolishing the entire school. Many houses in the village were damaged by the blast – the worst hit being the school caretaker's which was virtually destroyed.

Police and ARP wardens had been much too busy to erect any barriers so I spent nearly all day searching and collecting bomb fragments which I was able to swop and barter for bigger or better pieces. I kept one piece for many years as a permanent reminder of the visit to Grandma's and that long walk home.'

◙ RATIONING WENT ON ◙

'I suppose it must have been 1946, just after the war had ended. Anyway, I was still attending Reginald Street infants' school in Derby. One day our teacher told us that the next day we were getting a consignment of something from America and that we were all to take a tin with a lid on to school.

I took a National Dried Milk tin (a large one!). Each child's name was put on their tin and these were taken away. After school they were given back to us, lids firmly clamped on and we were instructed to take them straight home.

I went home through the Arboretum park. Halfway along the "back" path I just had to know what was in the tin so I prised off the lid – it was full of a light brown powder, too pale to be cocoa and which smelled like chocolate. I licked a finger and dipped it in; it was sweet and chocolatey – my first taste of drinking chocolate.'

HIGHDAYS & HOLIDAYS

HOME ENTERTAINMENT

Music and the radio were important to us, bringing entertainment into our homes. Many families will recall the pride felt in possessing their very own piano, and the pleasure they got from evenings round the radio – crystal sets, accumulators and all.

◈ OUR PIANO ◈

'When I was considered old enough my parents arranged for me to have piano lessons, which would cost one shilling per session. This was in the early 1930s.

After some months practising on Grandma's piano, Mother and Dad decided that we would have one of our own. They went to White's shop in Chesterfield and chose one which would cost £25 – an enormous sum. Dad's wages from the mine at Staveley were inadequate but, by careful budgeting and if Mother took in some washing jobs, the half-crown a week payments could be managed.

The piano was duly delivered and oh! what pleasure it brought, for Dad could play "by ear". Our little house was always full of my young aunts and uncles and their friends. The house rang with happy song. Meanwhile, I continued with my lessons.

Sadly, Dad did not live long enough to see an end to the piano payments. Mother's widow's pension was ten shillings a week plus five shillings allowance for me, now a ten year old. She battled on against poor health and worked hard to keep us both, doing housework and washing for others, but we were always well fed and clothed. Then one week, extra expenses stretched the budget too far and there was no half-crown to pay the "piano man" on his weekly visit. This distressed Mother who hated to admit defeat. Seeing how upset she was, I suggested that we go for a walk and avoid the caller. It went against the grain but

Mother was persuaded and off we went. Who was the first person we met? Yes, the piano man!

Mum struggled on and eventually our debt was paid and the piano was really ours. When I married she gave the piano to me. I will always treasure it because, apart from its weekly dose of Min cream and elbow grease, a great amount of love was invested in that piano.'

◙ DAD'S DRUMS ◙

'I lived in a small village called Two Dales, near Matlock. Dad was a musician and played the drums in Ron Farrell's Dance Band, going to the big houses and Smedley's Hydro in Matlock. In winter time when it was cold we had a small coal fire. The drums had to "sweat" to bring them up to temperature and had pride of place in front of the fire – we froze at the back of the room.'

◙ OUR FIRST RADIO ◙

'One of my brothers constructed our first radio which was a crystal set with a cat's whisker. We had headphones and a large pole outside held the wire for the aerial.'

◙ WIRELESS DAYS OF THE 1930S ◙

'I was born at the end of 1930, and my first 15 years of growing up are very vivid to me. My parents were in their forties when I was born, and I spent many hours with them happily listening to the wireless, which was still a new-fangled thing. First it was an accumulator set, the type where you had to take your glass batteries to be charged every week. Then we progressed to a Rediffusion Relay set, which came by land wire, and although you got perfect reception it didn't have a tuner, and so we were unable to whiz round the different stations to hear the "posh" voice of Radio Daventry and Droitwich, and the guttural sounds from Europe and Hilversum.

The wireless, as it was called in those days, was my window on the world. I remember very clearly standing with Mam in our kitchen on Remembrance Day, (which was always held on the

11th November and not the Sunday nearest as it is now) and wondering why Mam cried, but it was only ten or fifteen years since the ending of the Great War, and it was still so fresh in her memories, of all the friends and neighbours who had been killed.

I could sing all the programmes' signature tunes, from Henry Hall's *Here's to the next time* to *In Town Tonight*. I was amazed every week when the announcer could stop all that London traffic with just one "Sto-o-op". Do you remember *It's Monday Night at Eight o'clock*: the gravelly voice of Syd Walker and his song *Any old rags, bottles or bones*, and Ronnie Waldeman's Puzzle Corner, surely the forerunner of all the many quiz shows we see and hear today. Do you remember *Bandwagon* with Arthur Askey and Stinker Murdoch, and Arthur's girlfriend Nausea Bagwash? Do you remember the Kentucky Minstrels and how their conductor would say to them, with much shaking of the tambourines, "Gentleeme-e-e-en, be seated"?

Do you remember the stirring sound of the *Coronation Scot* every week heralding another exciting episode in the life of Paul Temple and his wife Steve; she was played by Marjorie Westbury and I thought she had the loveliest voice on radio. Do you remember *Children's Hour* – Larry the L-l-l-lamb and friends, Romany and his dog Rac, Harry Helmsley and his "children", and his famous catchphrase after much unintelligible gurgling from the baby: "What did Horace say, Winnie?" I remember Dad coming home early while I was listening to *Children's Hour*. After it was over he said, "That Uncle Mac and Auntie Doris sound all right, but that Auntie Muriel sounds a bit of a flibberty-gibbet." Well, for weeks after I would repeat this word under my breath. I thought it was a swear word.

My abiding memory of these "Wireless Days" is of a cosy living kitchen, curtains drawn against the autumn night, lovely coal fire roaring in the range, and me sitting with my mam and dad, picking at a pomegranate fruit with a pin. What happy, untroubled days they were to me.'

■ THE ACCUMULATOR ■

'The accumulator stood on the shelf next to the wireless,

connected inside somehow to the battery. The problem was that it only lasted a few days before it needed recharging. We had two accumulators, one large, one small, costing sixpence or threepence respectively to be charged up. The recharged large accumulator always had to be in position, working, for the Saturday night football results and later, *In Town Tonight*.

Then, late one Saturday afternoon, elder sister was going with her friends to the first house of the Victory Cinema, no time to fetch the dreaded accumulator. Mum was busy cooking dinner, Dad would soon be home, all eyes on me, yes I could do it (they said), after all it did have a steel carrying case and if I carried it very steadily so as not to spill the acid on my dress or legs (they said), and I was a sensible girl (they said). I was bribed with four halfpennies; twopence was a fortune! Down the hill I went with my big sister and her friends to the accumulator shop to take the small one in and pay sixpence for the big one, safely in its carrying case, and I was seen safely back across the road. I will never forget that walk home, not because I was a small child walking alone, no one seemed scared in those days. No! it was the dreaded accumulator and I for the next few years became part of the "Accumulator Brigade". So it was to be until electricity came to our area after the Second World War, when the battery and accumulator were dumped.'

Royal Celebrations

Royal occasions have always been celebrated with enthusiasm in Derbyshire towns and villages – and none more so than the Coronation of Queen Elizabeth II in 1953.

▣ Baslow Celebrates the 1935 Jubilee ▣
'On 6th May 1935 Baslow, like every other town and village, celebrated King George V's Silver Jubilee. I remember my father

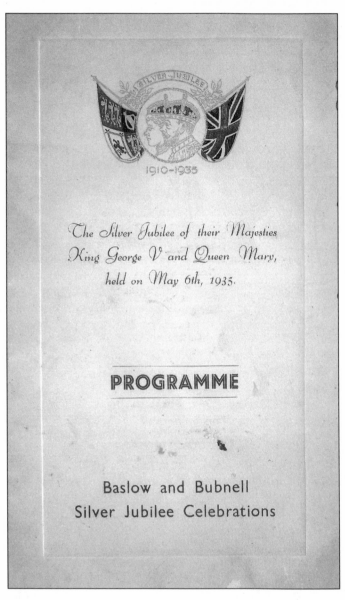

The Silver Jubilee of their Majesties
King George V and Queen Mary,
held on May 6th, 1935.

PROGRAMME

Baslow and Bubnell
Silver Jubilee Celebrations

Baslow's Jubilee celebrations included a five mile race.

taking part in the "marathon" in the senior sports. They ran about five miles in Chatsworth Park, starting from the Recreation Field, into the village of Edensor, across by the "House" to Queen Mary's Bower, returning to the Rec by the Park.

At the beginning of the race George Brightmore and Arthur Atkinson trailed the field. They were pacing each other, taking turns to lead. This worked well and as the spectators cheered, they were in the first three through the Kissing Gate leading back to the Recreation Field. Arthur shot ahead, arriving triumphant on the field, and stopped – only to be passed by George who remembered that a final lap of the Rec was required and thus came home first!

Another highlight of the day was the tug of war won by the Baslow team, with their fascinating nicknames of Kippy, Cocky, Gulger, Rough Judd, Straw Ben and Sampy.

The police sergeant in Baslow called his newborn daughter Sylvia Julie in honour of the occasion.'

◈ THE DAY KING GEORGE DIED ◈

'It began as a perfectly ordinary day, in fact I'm not quite sure which day of the week it was. It was February, a gloomy month, and I went to school as usual.

In those days there were no televisions in schools and the radio, a big square box with a round perforated screen in front, was only used for schools programmes, so for most of the day our school was cut off from the big world.

However the headmaster, Mr Dodd, went home for lunch. He came back looking very strange and we were called in from the playground at least five minutes early.

The screen was rolled up, just like "prayers" and Mr Dodd stood in front of us. In a quiet voice he said he had some very bad news. King George was dead, Princess Elizabeth was now our Queen and little Prince Charles (he wasn't yet four) was now heir to the throne. We said a prayer for King George and our new Queen, then went to afternoon lessons.

At home the television was not broadcasting. All that could be

Phyllis.

HIS MAJESTY THE KING'S SILVER
JUBILEE, 1935.

LONGFORD CELEBRATIONS.

Longford, like every other town and village, celebrated in 1935.

seen on the screen was the BBC coat of arms with the motto,
"Nation shall speak peace unto Nation".

About half past six my father came home. I ran to him crying,
"Have you heard the news?"

"Yes," he said, "Isn't it awful?" He bent down and pulled me
into his arms. "I'm so sorry for Lizzie," he said. "She's so young
for all that awful responsibility."

I didn't know then what he meant. After all for me, not quite
nine, Princess Elizabeth at 26 was grown up. Years later I did
understand. At 34 my father had been left a widower with a
newborn baby girl. He knew all about responsibility.

I remember a few days later seeing the new Queen, all in black,
emerging from the plane to be met by Sir Winston Churchill. On
our television we saw King George's coffin carried into the

chapel at Windsor, and a year later, the splendour of the Coronation of Queen Elizabeth II.

It is more than 40 years ago, but I shall never forget the day King George died.'

◈ CORONATION COACHES ◈

'With no village hall in Millers Dale there was nowhere to have a celebration meal on Coronation Day until it was suggested that the railway be approached to shunt a restaurant car into the siding. They agreed and also managed another coach with a hot axle-box, ideal for brewing up – all at a cost of £1.

The whole village participated in the various activities which included fancy dress for the children, decorated houses and sports. We all contributed to the cost of the meal by paying one

A railway restaurant car saved the day at Millers Dale in 1953 and the village gathered for a celebration Coronation meal.

shilling each per week for a period before the day. The actual Coronation was watched by everyone on the first television in the village.'

▨ A GREAT DAY ▨

'The day started grey and wet, but that did not dampen the excitement felt by everyone all over the country. It was the 2nd June 1953. I was eleven and a half years old living with my parents in our semi-detached council house at Weston on Trent. The streets and houses were decorated with flags and bunting and shops displayed pictures of the Queen and the Royal Family.

We were particularly excited in our house, the reason being we owned a television set, the only one in our road I might add. By nine o'clock the house was beginning to buzz as relatives, friends and neighbours joined us to watch the Coronation live from London. Perhaps 30 to 40 people crowded into our living room. Throughout the proceedings everyone was glued to the screen, the ooh's and aah's and comments were numerous. The viewing was only briefly interrupted by cups of tea and sandwiches.

The other children and myself left the proceedings in the afternoon to attend a party at the local secondary school where we each received a commemorative mug (unfortunately I broke mine some years ago). I particularly remember the tables laden with sandwiches, cakes, jellies, blancmanges and orange squash. By this time the weather had brightened up and in our front garden the red, white and blue flowers made a very patriotic display.

Back in the house the talk was naturally of the day's events. Everyone agreed "they would not have missed it for the world" and that "television was amazing".

Later we joined the rest of the town for a firework display and bonfire followed by more food and drinks at home. The euphoria stayed with us but by the end of the day I was glad to go to bed. Needless to say, the topic of conversation for the next week was a blow by blow account of the televised event.

That was over 40 years ago and these days televised special events are commonplace. But for the pleasure given to those few people it is still talked about today, and looking at the same road where I lived it has not changed much except every house now has a television aerial.'

▣ WE WERE THERE ▣

'One of my most memorable days was when I represented the Derbyshire Division of the Girls' Life Brigade (later the Girls' Brigade) at the Coronation of Queen Elizabeth II in June 1953. My friend and I, two 17 year olds, were chosen from the county's members.

On Coronation Eve we were taking part in Derby's celebrations on the Bass Recreational Ground, when members of youth organisations in the town provided a "royal" display. We then took a late evening train and stayed the night with a relative in London.

Early next morning we met up with the rest of the GLB contingent, girls like us who had travelled from all over Britain, proud to be there, to witness this historic event. As we paraded to our positions opposite Buckingham Palace the atmosphere was electric. As if the papers didn't have excitement enough with a Coronation to report, the billboards were announcing the conquest of Everest by Hillary and Tensing. What a day to achieve the ultimate!

The weather wasn't up to the occasion, but who cared? No one minded the rain. We stood – and sat – and stood – and sat, watching the processions and following all the comings and goings to and from the Palace, and thoroughly enjoying the pageantry. We had a spot just outside St James's Park and the Queen's procession went out to Westminster Abbey the other way, so we had to wait until it returned to get our good views.

It was such a long while, but time did not drag. We were *there*, other people had to be content with the wireless or TV if they were lucky enough to own one in 1953.'

ALL THROUGH THE YEAR

Every year brought its regular programme of events, from fairs and fetes to Bonfire Night and Christmas revels. A few people could afford holidays away from home, but for most families local celebrations gave a welcome break in the working year.'

❖ SHROVETIDE GAMES ❖

'We all remember Pancake Day for various reasons, to me it meant whips and tops and delicious pancakes with oranges and lemons. A few years later I was introduced to Shrovetide Football by my mother, an Ashbourne native. This game, played at Ashbourne, goes back hundreds of years and is still played with almost religious fervour on Shrove Tuesday and Ash Wednesday.

The game is between the Up'ards and the Down'ards, sides chosen by your birthplace in relation to the Henmore brook, the Up'ards being born north of the brook, the Down'ards to the south. There is no pitch, play can go just about anywhere and covers large distances, the goals being three miles apart. The Up'ards play to Sturston Mill and the Down'ards to Clifton Mill, these being the goals, the Henmore running down the centre of the playing area.

The rules are that the ball is turned up in Shawcross, the person who goals the ball keeps it as a souvenir, and no mechanical means of transport should be used to carry the ball, that's about it. By the way, roads in the town centre are closed to traffic during play.

A "hug" usually forms round the ball, as each side tries to force play towards the opposing goal. The movement of the hug is totally unpredictable, this explains why the local shops have their windows securely boarded up to avoid damage.

A good deal of the play is in the Henmore and the lake in the

A pre-war Shrovetide gathering at Ashbourne.

park, where participants seem to enjoy a good soaking, often staying in the water for long periods. The ball can break away from the hug in a running scrum through the town, or it may disappear for a time, often turning up at a goal hidden under someone's coat.

Royalty have been associated with the game over the years and have "turned up the ball" on several occasions. This task is also carried out by local dignitaries, and to be asked is considered a great honour. The beautifully decorated balls used in play are locally made from leather filled with cork; specimens from past years can be seen in the bar of the Green Man.'

'There have been changes in the game of Shrovetide over the last 50 years. The first change you notice is in the clothes they wore then – steel-capped boots and clogs and the roughest of clothes whereas now they wear running shoes and wet suits.

Now you see young lads of twelve playing. Fifty years ago it was much rougher and children would not be seen in the hug or the water. One thing that sticks in my mind is men taking out their dentures and handing them over to their wives or girlfriends before entering the battle. It *was* a battle in those days. Fights were taking place every few minutes. Women carried a bottle of scotch or rum to give to husband or boyfriend.'

'Clifton Mill in the 1920s was farmed by Mr F. Harrison. It was brick built with living accommodation, cow sheds and pigsty and stable. Over the mill race there was a three foot wide footbridge leading to the footpath to Dales Farm. There was a mill wheel over a 20 foot sluice where the Down'ards goaled the Shrovetide football. After the building was dismantled a memorial stone was erected to be used as the Clifton goal until 1995 when a new stone-built goal was erected on the river bank for future use.

In days gone by there was great interest in Shrovetide at Clifton with the goal being at the mill. After the ball was goaled the followers would congregate at the Cock Inn to relate the happenings of the day. Daisy Waywell, a well known local character, would be there too, following the ball for many years.

In 1906 a Shrovetider from Yeaveley goaled the ball at Clifton, taking it to Hollies Farm afterwards for a celebration after which he left with the ball to return home. Later he was found dead on the banks of the Henmore river just opposite the school. He was named as Bill Tunnicliffe and it was thought that he died from exposure.

Mr Frank Harrison was quite a character too. He farmed at the mill for a considerable time. He kept pigeons. His grandson recalled a very fast pigeon was entered in a race from Calais. It would not go into the loft but perched on a pole. This so infuriated Frank that he shot it – put it through the trip wire because it was the first back and took it to the Ashbourne Club and was disqualified. Well as his grandson said, "They couldn't have a dead pigeon winning the race could they?"'

◘ LITTLE EATON FAIR ◘

'Sometime before Easter new faces would appear at the village school. This would be the first sign of an exciting few weeks for the children of the village. The fair had begun to arrive! Each day more caravans would park on the road at the side of the New

Inn. Some of these caravans were very large and luxurious and spotlessly clean. The women must have had a hard time keeping them so with none of our modern conveniences. However, this was not in our minds as children and we eagerly watched the fair being erected on the coal yard at the rear of the New Inn.

The landlord at the time was also a coal merchant and kept his store of coal at the back of the pub. This was all cleared away for the fair which would open on Good Friday. We would look forward to the Thursday before, as this was testing day and the rides were free! On Good Friday itself the village was transformed, buses would run from Derby every few minutes doing a circuit of the village to take people back after their visit. We lived on the Duffield Road and it was busy with people walking from the next village. Our mothers all laid in a good stock of tea and cakes as someone was sure to call. The fair lasted for three days, not opening on Sunday in those days. On Tuesday the fair had gone before breakfast and the village returned to normal.

There is no longer a Little Eaton Fair, the pub has been enlarged and turned into a modern eating house, with houses now standing on the coal yard.'

◙ EASTER FROLICS ◙

'More years ago than I care to remember I was born and brought up in the then little village of Milford.

Every Good Friday it was the Annual Push Ball Match; all the money raised was for the Derby Royal Infirmary. A large ball about six feet high was pushed around the village by two teams of men dressed as women, though the numbers of players each side had was immaterial, the more the merrier. All the children were highly delighted and followed them around, and many adults came as well. We eventually arrived at the local football field – how the winners were decided upon was always a mystery to me, it seemed to be a free for all, arms and legs flying in all directions.

Jollifications were culminated by us all going to the dance evening. The Push Ball winners were presented with a cup and the losers with an egg cup. The dance went on to the wee small hours and any resemblance to "Come Dancing" was purely incidental, but it was fun and a good time was had by all.'

◙ MAY FESTIVAL ◙

'The traditional May Day festivities and merrymaking of May Queens and maypole dancing are more reminiscent of village life, but May Day was celebrated year on year by dozens of children in Derby. In the first week of May, the Central Hall was home to the Band of Hope May Festival. During the preceding months children were recruited, mainly from Sunday schools in the Peartree and Normanton areas, and gathered for auditions, a very professional approach.

Rehearsals were held on Saturday afternoons at one of the church halls. I remember one final rehearsal in 1946 when Derby County were playing Charlton Athletic in the FA Cup Final. Everyone went wild when the surprise news filtered through that Derby had won. There was little rehearsing after that.

The youngest children must have been only three or four. These little ones were usually attendants on the Queens. The line of succession in this ceremonial was Flower Queen, Fairy Queen, May Queen and retiring Queen, and each required a retinue of flowers, fairies (cute little dumplings mostly), train bearers, crown bearers (usually a part for a boy) etc. The Queens were teenage girls who could sing, as they were required to render a solo, suitably summery or flowery.

The maypole dancing must have been a nightmare for the organisers, it was almost burlesque at times. Half the dancers appeared to have two left feet and absolutely no sense of rhythm. To produce the plaits and spiders' webs required great concentration, just as difficult for children then as it is now. But generally the desired effect was produced on the day, the audiences were kind and overlooked the dropped braids and mistakes in the finished patterns.

The older children were mainly involved in the "Play", usually a traditional tale with music, a little like pantomime with comic characters alongside a leading lady and principal boy.

Dressed up for the May Festival in Derby.

There was great competition for parts and a high standard was expected and attained. I remember playing the role of Goldilocks which required the wearing of a beautiful golden wig with ringlets (I always had short dark straight hair) and a long pale green broderie anglaise dress. Glamour indeed! Another year I was Prince Charming in the Cinderella story.

We literally experienced the smell of the greasepaint. A team of ladies turned up on the night to apply the makeup and it was great to go home on the bus with it still on, and perhaps leave a trace or two till next morning to go to school.

I wonder now how the spectacle was achieved, particularly the costumes. I was performing throughout the 1940s, a period of clothing coupons and financial hardships, and there must have been a great deal of scrimping and saving, make do and mend, and hand-me-downs. I know my maypole dress doubled up as my Sunday school Anniversary dress.

For many children this would be their only chance to tread the boards and be in the limelight. This was, too, the first taste of theatricals for those who went on to join one of the operatic or drama groups in the town.'

❖ WELL-DRESSING ❖

'The origin of well-dressing is to give thanks for water. There are two stories of how it came about. The first is that the pure water from the wells at Tissington preserved the villagers during the Black Death of 1348-49. The second story is of a prolonged drought during the year 1615 when no corn or hay could be harvested during that dry summer.

The beginning of well-dressing was simple – boughs from trees and garlands of flowers were strewed around. Years ago the designs were quite simple but colourful. As a child Ascension Day, on which our Well-dressing has always been held, was a red letter day. We had a week off school as most of the children helped in various ways such as gathering flowers, spruce and such things.

My family were involved for many years. My grandfather, uncle and brother all designed wells and later my daughter and son's wife. My daughter-in-law designed the Yew Tree Well for over 20 years. We had a great many people come from all over the county. The railway ran trains that brought a lot of people into the village.

It was quite simple at first. We usually had another vicar come to preach the sermon. Often someone local, as there were very few cars in those days. When Sir William Fitzherbert became a baronet in the 1930s, his wife was a keen church lady. She formed a choir. A number of clergy took part – at least one for each well for the service. Each one took a short service at each of the wells.

We had quite a large fair too. That was held by the side of the school and pond. It was very exciting as we had a new outfit. After we had been to church we had to go and change into our other clothes before we could go on the fair.'

▣ GARDEN PARTY ▣

'One of the highlights of summer was the garden party given by Sir Herbert and Lady Wragg at Bretby House. Everyone who lived in Bretby and Stanhope Bretby went. Many have memories of a beautiful garden laid out to give great enjoyment to every age, clock golf, a treasure hunt, a beautiful baby competition and, most of all, a sumptuous tea during the years of rationing.'

▣ SUMMER HOLIDAYS ▣

'Dad was a fitter at Ireland Colliery, Staveley. In the 1920s his pay was six shillings and elevenpence per shift, working three days one week, four days the next. Mother never saw two pound notes together in any of his pay packets. Money was very scarce but, through Mother's careful management, we were able to afford a week in Blackpool each year. From the Yorkshire Penny Bank we had a money box which held exactly £5 when full. Mother used to say that if we could fill it in the year then we could go away. This source of saving was supplemented by savings in twopence-a-week chance clubs. You paid your money each week for a year but when you could have your money out depended upon your luck in the draw. It was usually arranged that we got our turn in time for the holiday.

Two suitcases were packed to capacity, one with clothes for Dad, Mother and myself, the other was heavy with food. We even took peas and beans from Dad's garden so that, when we arrived, we would not have to spend much money on food. Our apartment in Blackpool was booked at Mrs Turner's who would cook the food for us. We enjoyed the delights of sand and sea but we also sampled all the pleasures of the town – the Tower, the Circus, the Palace, Winter Gardens and Pleasure Beach: £5 went a long way in those days.'

◈ WAKES WEEK ◈

'Wakes Week was the big event of the year at Tideswell in the 1920s and we all took part in the Walks. The chapel congregation walked on Tuesday and the Church of England on Thursday, when we all had new hats. Joe Dale, the Town Crier, let us all know in good time what was going to happen as he did right through the year – what was happening and when, who had lost what and so on, it was a big network.

In Wakes Week there was so much going on. There was always a visit from the travelling fair which pitched in Market Square, a cricket match up at the ground at the Anchor crossroads, and of course, the grand finale was the horse racing up on the Cliff. A Mr Needham had a horse called Peaceable which we supported and my aunt Rose Langham made the teas for the spectators in a pavilion which is still up there. A gypsy had once come to the King's Head where she worked and had told her fortune: "You'll hold up your apron and money will rain into it." This sounded wonderful and when the horse races came round each year that's just what she did when she collected the money for the teas!'

◈ STAVELEY FEAST ◈

'On the weekend nearest to 24th June, the feast of John the Baptist, the fair came to Staveley. It was never known as a Fair, always a Feast. Held on the recreation ground (a grand name for a piece of unused land covered with black grit and ashes from

Derby carnival day in the late 1940s.

the nearby colliery), this was the event of the year for many.

In the local Speedwell infants' school, which overlooked the "rec", excitement grew to a fever pitch on the Thursday and Friday as we heard the huge wagons rolling in. We couldn't see them of course because the high windows and eight foot high wall round the school ensured that no outside distractions took our minds off our work. The luckier children lived in the "Terraces" near the fairground. After school ended they could watch the strange, brightly coloured vehicles arriving accompanied by their owners dressed in equally strange and colourful clothing. Local youths would offer their services around the feast ground in the hope of free rides.

At home, our mums would go in for an orgy of preparation. Special cleaning jobs were done, extra food bought and great batches of baking took place. Family and friends from far away would come to visit and take a walk to the Feast, returning with very dirty feet from the black grit underfoot.

Saturday night was teenagers' time. Girls with arms linked eyed the boys who were showing off on the rides. As darkness fell the roundabouts went faster and faster, squeals and music could be heard from miles away.

Sunday – and a feeling of desolation settled over the children. The wagons rolled away and the "rec" returned to its normal dirty, uninteresting state. The magic had gone.'

'Oh! the magic and delight of it all. As you entered the "rec" you came first of all to the stalls. Peteman, the pea man – ooh, the taste of those mushy peas and the mint sauce which became more vinegar and less mint as the time passed. There was the toffee man who made his spiel as he threw and pulled his toffee on a hook before pulling it out into long ropes and chopping it up into bite size pieces. There was the brandy snap stall and the stall where children could buy amusing small toys, the favourite one being the windmill-on-a-stick.

The roundabouts came next, first the "baby" ones, hand cranked. Then the bigger children were catered for with the Noah's Ark, the dodgems and Proctor's Peacocks whose steam organ was famous throughout the land.

There were the side shows where you might see the bearded lady or a two headed calf. The one favoured by the men was the boxing booth where the local likely lads would try their skill against the hard bitten fairground champions for a prize of £5 – only once known to have been won by a local.

The gambling instinct was well encouraged at stalls where you could roll a penny in the hopes of winning two or three; stalls where you could buy a ticket for a game of chance on an illuminated board – if you were lucky and the light came to rest on the same name as that on your ticket, you might win a much-to-be-treasured prize of toys or household goods.

Pervading all was the smell of the traction engines which were used to drive all the machinery and the cacophony of sound – blaring music from the roundabouts, the cries of stallholders and the incessant clang of the hard balls of the coconut shy banging against the metal sheet at the back.

Oh, the magic wonder of it all to a small child, clutching the few pennies so carefully hoarded during the preceding weeks and so quickly squandered in the fairground wonderland.'

Other treats were outings to Dovedale to cross the famous stepping stones.

◈ FINNEY'S FAIR ◈

'The days seemed longer, the skies seemed bluer and the long summer holiday stretched into the distance in the 1950s when we were young. We didn't need the telephone or the wireless to spread news, especially good news, it circulated the village as if blown by the breeze.

"Finney's Fair was on Smith's Field", on the corner of Brackley Gate and Quarry Road, Morley. We all sat on the wall of the field screwed up with anticipation as the various mysterious shapes began to turn into a coconut shy, rifle range, roll-a-penny (a big brown penny, that never quite fitted into the squares that meant you could win a crinkly ten shilling note). A small roundabout finished off this amazing picture that was painted before our eyes. The brightly coloured awnings, looking back, were perhaps not quite as bright as I remember, and the richness of the surroundings was probably very poor, but seen through the eyes of children they appeared to hold an Aladdin's cave of treasures.

Money was short and times were not easy. Many of the villagers were working on local farms or in other low paid work, so the excitement of "Finney's Fair" to our parents must have been rather muted and the constant call for "Just sixpence, Mum and we'll be really good, forever and ever", must have fallen on very weary ears. One benefactor always appeared at this time in the guise of the local roadman. Mr Gell could not have been a wealthy man and he lived with his "little wife" in a tiny cottage at the side of the field where the fair was held. Every year, just as our requests for money started to fall on deaf ears, Mr Gell called on Mr Finney with a whole pound note for us children to have a free "go" on everything the fair had to offer, except for some reason the rifle range.

The free goes were only allowed in the afternoon and we were not permitted to go to the fair in the evenings. Eight o'clock bedtimes were the norm for all of us. As we lay in our beds in the long light August evening we could hear the curly, whirly, tinny noise of the fairground organ. We could not help but wonder why we could not go in the evening when the adults did. What things did they get up to that were not for our eyes and ears?

Mr and Mrs Finney had a daughter who was around our age

A warm summer in Mickleover.

and we all hung on to her every word as she told us of her life travelling from village to village and town to town. Of how her sister had married "people like us" and that her parents no longer spoke of her. We would lie in the long warm strawlike grass and envy her missing school and changing school so often that she never had time to do all her lessons. She would get quite angry with us when we spoke of how lucky she was and how we wished we could live like her.

Those few days of "Finney's Fair" were the highlight of our summer holidays. An exotic episode, that now takes on all the aspects of a dream.'

◈ BONFIRE NIGHT – NOVEMBER 1938 ◈

'November, the month when coal fires were stoked high and rugs pushed against the bottom of doors to ward off the penetrating draughts, while outside the fog would descend, rising smoke from the chimneys aiding and abetting its clammy density. Upstairs the beds, heated by old stone hot water bottles, were the only warm spots in the rooms, and I can remember awakening on winter mornings to see the inside of the bedroom window etched over with frosty patterns! Mother's observation that Jack Frost had been at the window again was not appreciated as we stampeded downstairs to surround the fire, blessing the fact that Dad, through necessity, was an early riser and always had the fire roaring away by breakfast time. Grandad remained in bed until the first rush was over and his leisurely day could begin.

The first social event of the month was of course Bonfire Night when we congregated with the neighbours around the fire blazing at the bottom of the garden. Mother's contribution was a large quantity of sticky Bonfire Toffee boiled up in the old heavy saucepan then poured into large flat tins, to be broken up when set by Dad with a small hammer. Sandy, our dog, would pounce on the splinters of toffee that flew in various directions as the hammer descended on the slab. Grandad said Sandy was never disturbed by the noise of the exploding fireworks as he was too busy trying to remove the sticky toffee from his teeth, a problem shared by many as the evening wore on!

One item of clothing that Mother deemed essential for outdoor wear for winter activities in general and Bonfire Night in particular was the quaintly named pixie hood. This was made by folding a long woolly scarf in the centre and sewing the side edges together at one end to form the hood, whilst the long ends were wrapped around the neck. In addition to this, to protect my chest from the cold night air, another long scarf was criss-crossed over my coat and tied in a bulky knot at the back. This rendered me practically immobile from the waist up, and anything less like a pixie would be difficult to imagine! However, as the evening wore on and the bonfire blazed higher these minor hindrances were forgotten in the excitement as the fireworks exploded; the Catherine wheels nailed to the garden fence flew round and round as the Roman candles and pom-poms lit up the sky whilst Racketeers flew along erratically at ground level causing great hilarity!

As the bonfires died down and the fireworks dwindled we

little thought that by November 1939 we should be enveloped by the blackout and that for the next six years the fires lighting up the skies over England would be of a very different character.'

⊞ BONFIRE NIGHT IN THE 1950S ⊞

'The first Bonfire Nights that I recall were in a corner of the apple orchard and family and friends would come to our farm in Longford. For weeks before any old wood would be piled there, then on the night when everyone was assembled we would leave the warmth of the kitchen and go through the little gate to the orchard to light the fire and later the fireworks.

One year my sister and I decided to try potatoes baked in the fire. We got the potatoes from the clamp and put them in an old frying pan, I think, and put them at the edge of the fire, before it was lit. When we thought they must be cooked the fire was too hot to get close to. I think we misunderstood the instructions. The next day we found the unburnt (or melted) half of the frying pan but no potatoes.

After my mum died the party moved to Bupton House Farm, and two memories of Bonfire Night there are very strong. The bonfire was near the road and someone, or more than one person, decided to throw bangers over the hedge. When they came back and threw some more later in the evening one of the

farmers was waiting with a bucket of pigswill and threw it over the hedge at them. It was agreed it would be known who was throwing the bangers by how they smelt next day.

The other memory is of Maureen putting on her new small record, that she had only had that day. I had not seen a 45 rpm record before, only 78s, so it looked rather small. Then into the room where we youngsters were eating came this new music that made us want to dance. Maureen showed us how to rock and roll to this record and we didn't want to stop. We got so warm we spilled out into the garden and didn't want to go home. The record was Cliff Richard's *Move It*. My first taste of "pop music".'

❂ CHRISTMAS IS COMING ❂

'Just before Christmas, before the war, we were taken to Sheffield to have a look at what we might like to have for Christmas. In those days we got just one special present, plus an orange, apple, new penny and sweets. Woolworths was still a 3d and 6d store then, and after looking round we would be given a special treat by going to the store cafeteria for rissoles and chips.'

❂ CAROL SINGING ❂

'Before 1914 we children at Tintwhistle would go to carol singing on Christmas Eve, starting at Mrs James' in Millbrook. We used to wait till the clock struck midnight and then sing the first carol. We would sing round the village all night. Our leader had a pocket full of raisins to give us to make us sing. Then we'd finish up at the last house about six o'clock in the morning for breakfast. Afterwards we would go to bed till the Christmas dinner was ready.'

'One Christmas when I was eight years old our family and others from the Methodist chapel in Longford went carol singing with a piano on the back of one of my Dad's lorries. We had a paraffin lamp to read the music by. We drove round Longford singing our hearts out, eating mince pies and drinking anything we were given. That's why Ginty (aged five) and I were disappointed to be left with Mr and Mrs Old at the post office while the rest of the party went to sing at the Ostrich pub.'

◉ CHRISTMAS 1956 ◉

'Christmas 1956 – I awoke when it was still dark or was it? Yes, it was dark but there was a strange silence and an eerie light and it was cold – so cold – no central heating in 1956 – however did we manage it? What was this lovely feeling I had? Excited! Expectant! What was it? It was Christmas Day! I leaped out of bed and felt for the pillowcase that I'd left empty when I went to bed, was it only last night, on Christmas Eve? Now is was full of lumpy, bumpy parcels all wrapped up in crinkly paper with that special Christmassy smell. I could just make out a box of Maltesers on the top so I opened them greedily and stuffed in a mouthful – nothing like illicit chocolate! I realised that I was getting chilly and looked out of the window. Beautiful frost patterns had to be cleared from the inside of the pane and there was the snow – it had fallen thickly overnight covering the road and pavement of the street outside our palisaded house in Peartree, Derby. A perfect Christmas morning.

It was actually about 7 am but it seemed much earlier and Mum allowed me into her and Dad's room after my fourth plea of, "Is it time yet?" A fire was burning in the grate specially for Christmas Day – we only had a fire upstairs if someone was ill usually and it gave a lovely glow to the proceedings.

As an only child Christmas always seemed very special as there was only me to please and the pleasant task of unwrapping the parcels began in earnest. New slippers followed exciting board games and books, always books. I also loved music and that year Dad had bought Mum a portable Dansette record player – guess who had the most use of that? Another gift was a long playing record of the soundtrack of *Kismet* starring Howard Keel and Dolores Grey. We had recently been to see this gorgeously flamboyant musical round the corner at the Normanton Picture House and I had been most impressed by Miss Grey's glamorous gold costume and Afghan hounds and I was to spend most of Christmas Day parading round in old net curtains with a reluctant, less exotic mongrel as my faithful hound pretending to be dancing in the deserts of Arabia to the strains of *Not Since Ninevah*. At least it kept me warm!

I also found the time to play in our long, narrow garden in the

215

snow with Cinders, my dog, now blissfully rushing about instead of being part of my Kismet act, and to build a snowman with Dad while Mum cooked the lunch, the treat of the year, chicken!

After a quiet afternoon playing with my new things in the front room, again specially warmed by a fire, it began to get dark about 3 pm and it was time to go up to my Nana's house about a mile away in a straight line up the long streets with two or three road junctions and a main road to cross.

1956 was a safer haven for children. I was allowed to pack a brown paper carrier bag with string handles with a book, a bag of sweets, my doll with two changes of clothes, a game and a colouring book and crayons along with new slippers. I was then wrapped up warmly in coat, gloves, scarf and wellingtons, given the dog on a lead and sent off alone on our Arctic expedition to Nana Gladys's home where assorted ancient relatives would be sitting in groups exclaiming on how I'd grown. I always wondered how they got there and where they went for the rest of the year as they only seemed to appear for Christmas Day tea. Mum and Dad came up about 6 pm and a gargantuan buffet tea was laid out to pick at all evening including Nana's legendary trifle with sherry! We played parlour games and Grandad always played the piano for a sing-song – no need for Christmas TV in those days. About 10.30 pm it was time to go as I was beginning to drop off to sleep in a chair and had to be slapped awake. The temperature had fallen and the snow was crisp to walk on. Dad carried me halfway home but I got my second wind and hopped, skipped and jumped through the snow for the other half. After a cup of Ovaltine made with milk I was ready to be tucked up into bed. What a lovely Christmas Day and what a happy, contented eight year old.'

▨ THE LAST CHATSWORTH PARTY ▨

'One afternoon after the Christmas holidays all the children from Baslow, Beeley and Pilsley schools and Sunday schools were taken by Hulley's buses to Chatsworth House.

There seemed to be lots of us. We were entertained by a

conjuror in the ballroom theatre, and then had tea and crackers in the Orangery (now the shop at Chatsworth). In another room, with a huge Christmas tree, sat the 10th Duke and Duchess of Devonshire. Our names were called out and we went up to the Duchess who gave us each a present. I remember a sewing set and being very shy. We all sang and gave three cheers for our hosts.

This must have been the last of the traditional parties in 1938.'

INDEX

LIST OF CONTRIBUTING INSTITUTES

*Contributions have been received from the following Derbyshire
Women's Institutes:*

Abney ● Alfreton ● Allenton ● Allestree ● Alvaston ● Ashbourne,
Barrow on Trent ● Barrowhill ● Baslow ● Beighton ● Belper ● Biggin,
Bolsover ● Brailsford ● Breadsall ● Bretby ● Burbage ● Carlton,
Carsington & Hopton ● Castle Gresley ● Cedars ● Chaddesden,
Chapel en le Frith ● Charlesworth ● Clifton ● Cromford,
Cumberhills ● Darley Abbey ● Darley Dale ● Etwall ● Findern,
Great Hucklow ● Hatton ● Hazelwood ● Higham & Shirland,
Hilton & Marston ● Hope ● Horsley & Coxbench,
Hulland & District ● Humbleton ● Kirk Ireton ● Littleover ● Loscoe,
Mickleover ● Millersdale & District ● Morley ● Mosborough,
Newton Solney ● Norbury & Roston ● Oakwood,
Ockbrook & Borowash ● Ockbrook Redhill ● Old Glossop ● Pentrich,
Ravensdale ● Repton ● Risley ● Rowsley & District ● Rowthorne,
Shipley ● Spondon ● Stanton by Dale ● Stapenhill ● Starkholmes,
Sudbury ● Sutton on the Hill ● Taddington ● Tibshelf,
Ticknall & District ● Tideswell ● Tintwhistle ● Tissington & District,
Turnditch & Windley ● Tutbury ● Uffa Magna ● Walton,
West Hallam & District ● Weston on Trent ● Whatstandwell,
Whittington ● Whitwell & District ● Willington ● Wingerworth,
Wingerworth Morning ● Wirksworth Morning,
Wirksworth Heritage ● Woodthorpe ● Wormhill ● Youlgreave.